University of Sheffield
School of Architecture

1908–2008

A Centenary History

by Peter Blundell Jones
Professor of Architecture from 1994

The University Of Sheffield.

The Alumni Foundation

Printed with the help of a grant from the University of Sheffield Alumni Foundation

The opinions are those of the author and do not reflect official policy of the University of Sheffield

Published by BDR Publications
The School of Architecture
University of Sheffield

ISBN: 978-0-9556536-1-2

Design and Layout Peter Blundell Jones
Cover design by Glenn Thornley

Printed and bound in Great Britain by
The University Print Service
Bolsover Street
Sheffield

Acknowledgements

Researching the first hundred years of our school made me feel I should have done it earlier, for despite having been in the school 13 years there was much that I did not know and some things about which I had been misinformed. Sifting through the evidence, I became deeply aware of how many dedicated staff had given their lives and energies to it, which elicited a new respect. Inevitably there will be missing figures and stories untold, especially about the early years, but the sheer quantity of information also made it a challenge to produce a coherent and balanced narrative, to decide what to put in and what to leave out. The selection of illustrations posed a particular problem, for early student drawings are scarce, so that for the pre-war years I had to use more or less all that I could obtain, whereas recent records are very full, creating an embarrassment of choice. I tried to present a balanced sample, where possible repeating selections already made by the school for its own publications or for awards, but where such precedents were lacking I preferred works by notable alumni and by students who had gone on to become members of staff. My starting point with the text was the work of Roger Harper, who joined the school in 1972 becoming one of its main historians, and retired as Reader in 2000. He has done more than anyone else to research the local Sheffield practices and has published a comprehensive history of the Sheffield Society of Architects and Surveyors (Roger H. Harper The first hundred years of the Sheffield Society of Architects 1887-1987 published by the Sheffield Society of Architects 1987) which I drew on extensively. Some material relating to the general university history (Helen Mathers Steel City Scholars, James and James, London 2005) was passed on by Clyde Binfield and Helen Mathers, for which I thank them. Hints on the early development of architectural education as a national phenomenon were provided by Andrew Saint and by Alan Powers, who wrote his doctoral thesis on that subject. Alec Daykin, who was a student in the school from the mid 1930s and a member of staff from 1947-1989, proved to be a mine of information and kindly gave his student drawings to the school. Bob Adams, a former partner of Hadfield Cawkwell and Davidson with many links to the school, provided specific material about Robert Cawkwell as well as filling in more background. Irena Murray of the RIBA dug up information on our first lecturer, W.S. Purchon, and about RIBA education meetings. Former professors John Page, Ken Murta and Peter Tregenza were generous with their time, as were two staff members who went on to professorships elsewhere: Austin Peter Fawcett and Geoffrey Broadbent. Alumni interviewed at length included John Allan, Philip Toft, Andrew Beard, Bill Taylor, Anne Minors, David Cash, Greg Penoyre, Stephen Proctor, Andrew Matthews, and Simon Allford. Additional thanks are due to John Allan and Philip Toft for use of drawings from their student portfolios. Current students interviewed included Shankari Raj, Sam Goss, Tom Vigar, Joseph Mackie and Jamie Wakeford. Alan Williams contributed some initial research, and Miles Stevenson of the alumni office shared their data. Tatjana Schneider kindly gave me access to her detailed research on the Arts Tower. Ruth Harman and the City Archive were helpful over photographing the early Cawkwell drawing and HCD with their permission. I should also thank the University Library and special collections for providing material and our archivist Matt Zawadski and heritage officer Anthea Stephenson for identifying it. Peter Lathey, our departmental photographer, tirelessly undertook much scanning and photography. Finally I should thank the current staff for many tips, suggestions and contacts, and my fellow professors Bryan Lawson, Jeremy Till and Roger Plank for allowing me the time and opportunity to pursue this task with complete editorial freedom.

Peter Blundell Jones September 2007

Architectural Education in Sheffield
Alternative Schemes

A A complete Scheme of three or four years Courses

Architecture & Architectural draughtmanship ⎫ At University

Mathematics, Physics, Literature ⎬ College

Art, Ornament, figure & life . . At School of Art

Surveying, Construction & Sanitation . . . At Technical School

A Professor of Architecture at University College who would also direct the Students generally as to their attendance at the other Classes

The Students to give to the Lectures and Classes whole time for first year or until they had passed the Preliminary Examination of the R.I.B.A., two thirds time until they had passed the Intermediate and one third time until they had passed Final Examination

This would necessitate the provision at the University College : –

A Class Room & Library about 30 ft × 20 ft with a Professor's Private Room and possibly also the use of one of the Lecture Rooms adjoining.

The cost would be at the least £500 a year which would have to be provided by the Profession either by obtaining donations for an endowment, or by annual subscriptions, or by Students Fees or a combination of the three.

The Profession might agree as to a minimum but sufficient premium and that the Master was to pay out of this premium all the Students Fees.

8

Edward Gibbs's proposal of 1903 for a school of architecture in Sheffield, page eight.

The first century of the University of Sheffield School of Architecture

is a story of growth from modest local roots to national and international importance in parallel with other disciplines. Taking in its first students in January 2008, the school started slightly later than the main founding departments of the university,[1] but its presence had been planned by 1903 and it remains among the oldest architectural schools in Britain (Architectural Association, London 1847, Liverpool 1895, Manchester 1903, Bartlett 1911, Birmingham 1909, Cambridge 1912).[2]

There had been schools abroad a century earlier, Paris's École Polytechnique (1795) and École des Beaux Arts (1819) setting the crucial precedents, but architecture in Britain relied until the end of the 19th century on the pupilage system, a form of apprenticeship in which a young man paid a not insubstantial fee to be articled to an architect,[3] did much tedious drawing and clerical work in his principal's office, and was supposed to absorb an education along the way, eventually joining the profession by passing the RIBA's exams. The weaknesses of this system were pilloried by Dickens through the architect Pecksniff in *Martin Chuzzlewit*, but Philip Webb and William Morris evidently received a valuable education this way in the office of G.E. Street, architect of London's Law Courts.[4]

It was at best haphazard, and the pupils were completely at the mercy of the principal, restricted by his distribution of tasks to them and limited to his knowledge and talent. An indenture document of 1910, presumably standard for the time, reveals just how one-sided this kind of contract could be. Robert Cawkwell (1894-1968),[5] later partner in the leading Sheffield firm Hadfield Cawkwell and Davidson, was articled to Arthur Nunweek for £80 (the equivalent today of £5,500 to £7,000).[6]

His mother, aside from paying this fee, bound herself to supply his board and lodging and any medical expenses that might accrue. In return he had to promise in some detail to do the work allotted to him, not to absent himself during office hours, to *'acquit and demean himself honourably, faithfully and with diligence'* and *'in all respects (to) conform to the rules of the office'*. He was bound *'not to do anything that will cause damage or injury to the Principal or his goods'*, with provision of compensation from his mother should he stray into any misdemeanours, yet Nunweek's side of the bargain was merely that he:

...shall and will according to the best of his skill power and knowledge during the said term of years teach and instruct, or cause to be taught and instructed, the said Robert Cawkwell in the said profession or business of an architect... with the object of enabling (him) to qualify himself for passing the examinations for studentship and associateship of the RIBA.[7]

There was no specified curriculum or hours of study whatsoever, though in the event Cawkwell was allowed to attend the part-time class at the university, and a drawing for a pair of cottages survives, the earliest example of student work yet found.[8] Further light is shed on those times by John Mansell Jenkinson, an early part-time teacher in the school who rose to take over the leading Sheffield firm of Hemsoll and Paterson. His memoir reveals the life and its technological limitations:

I was articled for five years in 1899 and was initiated into the mysteries of architectural practice by the office staff. These consisted of getting out their drawing boards and Tee squares in the morning and putting them away at 5.30 in the evening, writing out letters in long hand (there were no typewriters in our office at that time) and then copying them in a letter book. As there was no telephone, an accurate knowledge was obtained of the highways and byways of Sheffield by the delivery of messages and letters to the various offices in the neighbourhood. Plans were drawn in pencil on cartridge paper and then inked in and coloured. Tracings were made on linen for the corporation and further tracings for contractors, as photo-printing was only in its infancy. Specifications were written out by hand and cyclostyle copies were made. Usually these were separate for the various trades and competitive tenders were obtained for each. Bills of quantities were prepared by the principals and I never remember any being done in my pupilage days in our office by an outside quantity surveyor. As the staff had the job of carefully checking the mathematical side of the quantities, a comprehensive knowledge of what was included in the bill was automatically obtained. Part of the articled pupils' training was to visit the jobs in progress. The builders commenced work at 7.00 a.m. so there was sufficient time to spend an hour with them before breakfast and coming down to the office at 9.30. This was a very useful part of a young architect's training and the value of making a friend of the foreman has remained with me all my life.[9]

1. Drawing of Edward Gibbs by William Rothenstein, dated 1919.
2. (opposite) Presentation drawing of a design for cottages by Robert Cawkwell, 1911, executed in the school's evening class. (Sheffield City Archives)

Edward Gibbs and the Sheffield Society of Architects

A growing concern among leading practitioners about the limitations of the pupilage system led in the late 19th century to the founding of architectural associations and societies across Britain. These were dedicated to advancing the interests of the profession, promoting knowledge and debate, and helping young architects to get through the RIBA examinations. The Sheffield Society of Architects started relatively late in May 1887, but was immediately supported by all the leading local firms and had become allied to the RIBA by the end of 1888. It met in the offices of Flockton and Gibbs,[10] architects of the Mappin Art Gallery and later of the University's buildings, and the initial meeting included principals from the Flockton, Hadfield, and Helmsoll firms as well as Holmes & Watson, Innocent & Brown, Mitchell-Withers, and Webster.[11] The society raised a subscription and started a library which was kept at the School of Art in Arundel Street: there were a mere 42 books in 1900.[12] It organised basic lectures for pupils on mouldings and the orders, as well as local architectural visits and topical

SHEFFIELD · UNIVERSITY · DESIGN · CLASS
DESIGN · FOR · A · PAIR · OF · SEMI · DETACHED · COTTAGES

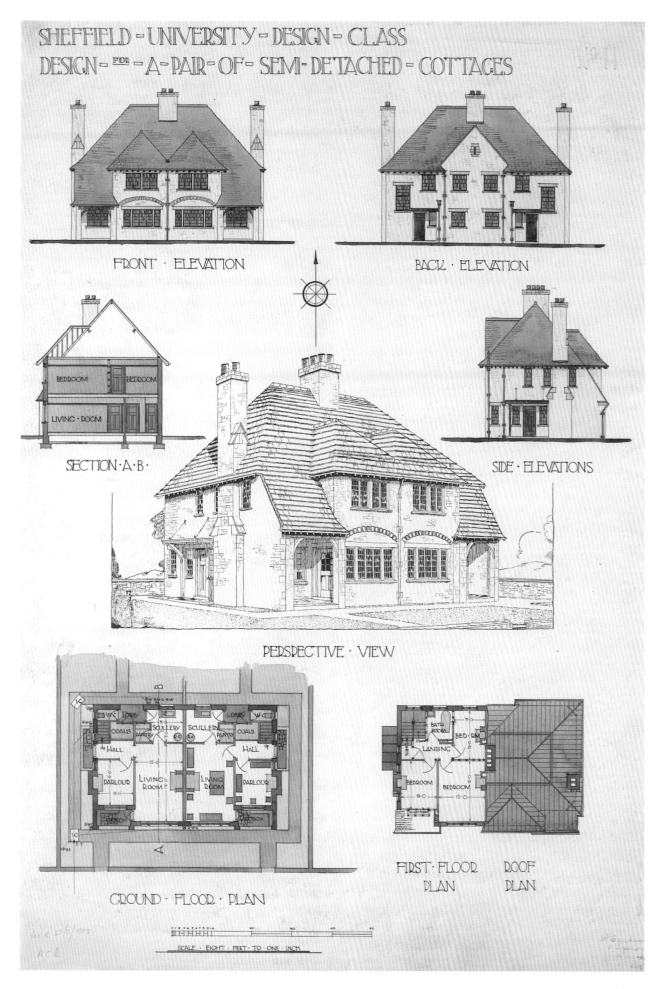

FRONT · ELEVATION

BACK · ELEVATION

SECTION · A · B ·

SIDE · ELEVATIONS

PERSPECTIVE · VIEW

GROUND · FLOOR · PLAN

FIRST · FLOOR   ROOF
PLAN   PLAN

SCALE · EIGHT · FEET · TO · ONE · INCH

7

presentations by outsiders: over 70 lectures by the turn of the century. There were sketching parties and classes from 1892, and design classes from 1893, but organising them on an evening and voluntary basis proved difficult and sporadic, and the society had to admit disappointment at a poor uptake in 1895-6.

Edward Mitchel Gibbs 1847-1935[13] (of Flockton and Gibbs) a leading Sheffield architect and the most active of the teachers, was seeking to establish these classes on a firmer footing when he proposed a national school of architecture in 1900.[14] There had already been discussions with Firth College in 1894 about instituting a Chair of Architecture which came to nothing, and in 1902 a further move was made to hold classes at the School of Art, but by then Gibbs was already at work on the planning of the new university buildings at Firth Court, and was inspired by the architectural schools he saw on an exploratory visit to the United States.[15] He saw inclusion within the new university as the solution, and was the instigator of a proposal from the Sheffield Society of Architects in 1903 that they be given a room in the new building and a lecturer. This was discussed in a meeting with the Senate Building Committee, and a detailed paper, *Architectural Education in Sheffield: Alternative Schemes,* signed by Gibbs in February 1903, charts the components of a three year course involving University College, the Technical School and the School of Art, assuming the presence of a professor.[16] In the working drawings for Firth Court of 1903, the galleried tower room that would become the department of architecture already existed, but it was labelled as the museum of biology, the department of biology being housed immediately below.[17] Whether Gibbs foresaw or even intended its conversion to the architecture school's purposes is unrecorded, but it could enjoy the toplight then considered essential for drawing, and its presence doubtless also helped justify the construction of an element crucial to his external composition. By November 1905, the society had agreed to support the school, and the necessary room was redesignated. The University Council ratified the administrative arrangements in May 1907, and in July the agreement between the Society and the University was published. The Society was to support the appointment of a Lecturer in Architecture at £200 p.a. for three years, making up to the university any shortfall on fees. Pledges were provided by the leading Sheffield architectural firms and by the RIBA.[18]

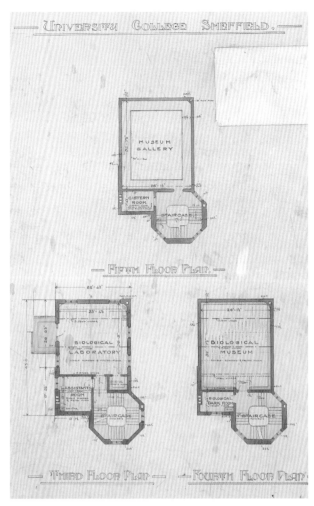

3. Upper plans of Firth Court as shown in the original drawings, with the 3rd floor Biological laboratory, the 4th floor intended Biological Museum, and its gallery.
4. (below) The tower as it appears today.
5. (opposite) Elevation and sections from the original set: the lower drawing shows the rooms in the tower.

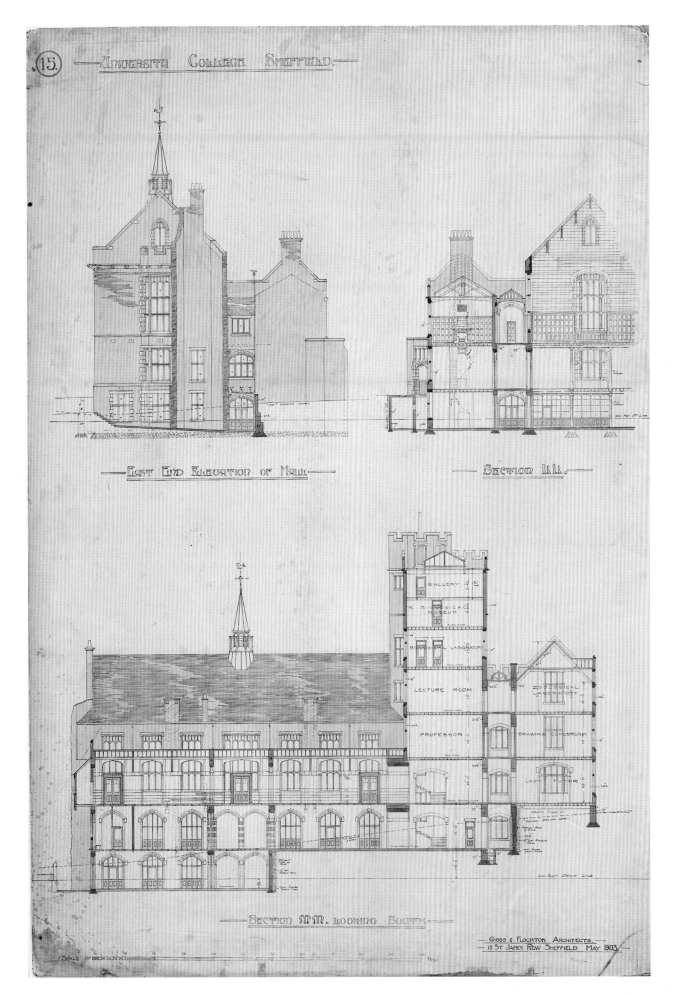

University College Sheffield.

East End Elevation of Main.

Section M.M.

Section M.M. Looking South.

GALLERY
BIOLOGICAL MUSEUM
BIOLOGICAL LABORATORY
LECTURE ROOM
ZOOLOGICAL LABORATORY
PROFESSOR
DRAWING CLASSROOM
LADY TUTOR

Gibbs & Flockton Architects.
15 St James Row Sheffield May 1903.

9

6. William Sydney Purchon, the first lecturer.

7. (below) Unity Church, Crookesmoor Road, 1915, designed by James Wigfull, one of the principal advisers in setting up the school. It is now student accommodation.

Modest beginnings with Purchon

William Sydney Purchon (1879-1942) was appointed as the first lecturer. He had been articled to an architect in Hull and studied there before moving on to the Battersea Polytechnic and Royal Academy Schools in London, then he had worked for the Admiralty Works Department for eight years.[19] The reason why Gibbs chose him at the age of 28 is not known. In preparation for the job he and Gibbs visited other British schools of architecture along with James Wigfull to see how things were done.[20] Wigfull was the architect of the brick Gothic Revival church in Crookesmoor Road and the Thomas Boulsover Memorial in Whiteley Wood. He was also active in the Hunter Archaeological Society, founded in 1912.[21]

The school started in January 1908 with four full-time students plus three in an evening class,[22] but within three months numbers had grown to six full-time and seven evening students. Not all of the teaching time was devoted to architectural subjects, as the first year curriculum included English, history, mathematics, physics, and chemistry, in order to matriculate. The main concentration in the architectural part seems to have been on drawing skills, both freehand and accurate drawing of 'ornament from the round', though there was also a lecture course in 'Ancient History'. The second year history course moved on to 'Outlines of Medieval and Renaissance Architecture in Europe'. This was accompanied by drawing of the orders and technical drawing, and there was much more about construction, including structure, sanitary science, mechanics, and chemistry of building materials. There were visits to building sites, measured drawings, and even working drawings – but no mention of design. Third year continued with technical subjects but emphasis on history increased, with 28 lectures on English architecture dealing with Romanesque, Gothic, and Renaissance, and another 28 on 'The Development of Architectural Features' including the temple plan, the vault and dome, supports and openings, ornament and sculpture. At last design was introduced, taking the two forms of 'domestic work' and 'academic work', but it seems even at this third year level not to have been the focus. A continuing 'special course' was provided for students wishing to progress further still into a fourth year and going on to attempt the RIBA finals. This concentrated on design projects, with 'written criticisms offered'.[23]

General courses towards matriculation and

technical courses were provided by other departments of the university, allowing the nascent school to remain small and thinly staffed, the calendar commenting that:

The lecturer is assisted in the work and supervision of the advanced course by leading members of the architectural profession in the city, and there are also courses by members of the staffs of the faculties of arts, pure science, applied science, and of the technical school of art.[24]

The purchase of £40 worth of books was guaranteed personally by Gibbs. The RIBA sent as a first visiting board Aston Webb and Halsey Ricardo, two leading national figures.[25] By 1910 the two year course was granted exemption from the RIBA intermediate examination and approved as providing a *'thorough grounding in architectural knowledge'*.[26] At the end of the first year the Society cleared a deficit of £138, and there was a smaller debt the following year, but by the outbreak of the First World War the Society was still subsidising the school to the tune of £25 p.a.. Little has survived to indicate Purchon's teaching ethos, but he seems to have been an Arts and Crafts sympathiser, for he was

8, 9. Two drawings from the Devey Collection, University Library. Above is a presentation study of a lodge in ink, below a quick elevation sketch of a cottage in pencil. They show Devey's love of the vernacular and penchant for irregular massing. The Devey collection was brought to Sheffield by Purchon.

11

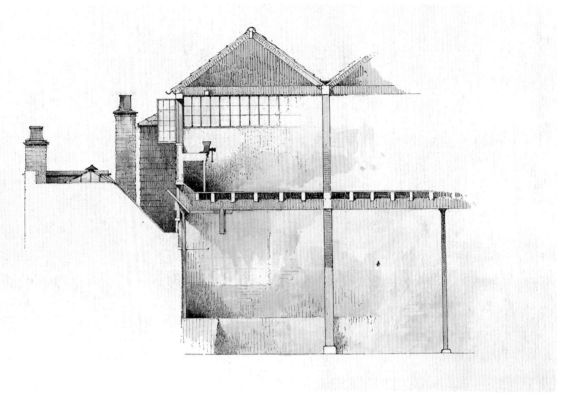

10, 11. Two more drawings from the Devey Collection. The watercolour above has a note 'rights of light, Shoreditch' and weak pencil outlines of the window section. It was evidently an investigation concerned with daylighting the lower room with a clerestory window, but it also shows the workshop above. Below is an elevation of the chapel at Killarney, a Devey country house.

12, 13, 14. (opposite) Three illustrations from C.J. Innocent's *The Development of English Building Construction*, Cambridge University Press, 1916: top, a traditional unglazed window; middle 'Barn at Cowley Manor'; bottom, joints at Millhouses. Innocent lectured in the school at the time of publication.

instrumental in bringing to Sheffield in 1914 a collection of sketches by George Devey (1820-1886) the master of C.F.A. Voysey, that is still in the University Library.[27] James Williams, Devey's partner, had been seeking a home for them, and Purchon guaranteed:

that they would not only be useful to me and my students, but that they would be highly appreciated by all in Sheffield to whom architecture means something more than a somewhat precarious way of making a living.[28]

He was evidently well acquainted with Devey's work, admiring him as *'an artist to his finger tips who thoroughly loved his work'*, and claiming him as the pioneer of 'the new movement' which embraced the work of Webb, Shaw, and Nesfield:

Architecture in England was frigidly cold classic or almost equally cold Gothic... Devey loved the work of the Middle Ages, but he was one of the first nineteenth century architects to perceive the charm of the work of our early Renaissance designers and the fact that a freer type of design might be more suitable to the requirements of this time than copies of Greek or Gothic... He was also a lover of the delightful cottages in English villages... [and] a master of the design of lodges and cottages... [which] harmonised so well with their surroundings that they have often formed the subject of sketches and photographs.[29]

Purchon received assistance from various quarters, the Calendar recording the presence of assistant lecturer James Miller in 1910-12 and John Mansell Jenkinson (principal in the Hemsoll firm) from 1912-16, both presumably part-time. Neither is credited with particular courses. A.C.C. Jahn and staff of the Technical School of Art taught Architectural Ornament, Gibbs taught evening classes in design, and history lectures were divided between prominent figures in local firms, Italian Architecture being covered by Henry Leslie Paterson (of the Hemsoll firm), English Architecture by John Brightmore Mitchell-Withers and Charles Frederick Innocent. The latter was the son of the Sheffield schools architect Charles J. Innocent[30] and author of *The Development of English Building Construction* published by Cambridge University Press in 1916, a landmark in vernacular architecture studies which included illustrations of old buildings in the Sheffield area, particularly timber-framed and cruck constructions.[31]

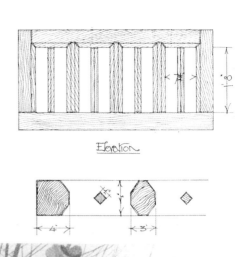

Elevation

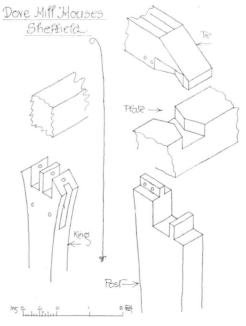

Dove Mill Houses Sheffield

The school had begun within the Faculty of Applied Science but in 1911-12 it was transferred to the Arts Faculty to allow development of a five year course leading to an arts degree with honours. This involved additional courses in arts subjects during the first year, the architectural content being reduced to three hours of lectures and three hours of tutorial per week. In 1914 Sheffield students gained two distinctions among five given nationally, and both were awarded to sons of leading Sheffield firms: Henry Gibbs (Edward Gibbs's son)[32] and Herbert Leighton. The latter returned immediately to the school as part-time 'junior lecturer and demonstrator' in 1915, and was later to become its longstanding construction lecturer, remaining until his retirement in 1960. The most notable alumnus from this early period was Charles Herbert Aslin, who completed his studies at the beginning of the First World War and taught in the school in the 1920s. He went on to become County Architect for Hertfordshire and the patron of the Hertfordshire schools movement.[33] He was also the first graduate of the school to become President of the RIBA: from 1954-56.

Though Purchon and his assistants had evidently been doing a good job with a constant eye to improvement and expansion, the war and its aftermath brought setbacks: student numbers shrank and the department was even temporarily closed.[34] A scheme to add a department of town-planning, involving the artist William Rothenstein who was made Professor of Civic Art in 1917, petered out after Rothenstein became Director of the Royal College of Art in London in 1920.[35] Purchon filled his time with war work for the steel firm Firth's, designing some laboratories and canteens and a works gateway that still exists in Savile Street East,[36] but in 1919-20 he was still on half-time, and senate minutes record his plea for at least £500 p.a. Frustrated, he sought to engage in private practice, and Vice-Chancellor Sir Henry Hadow actively supported the idea, but the Sheffield Society of Architects protested that *'Professors and lecturers at the university should not compete with men in private practice,'*[37] even if restricted to small jobs. Purchon left in 1920, precipitating the school into a crisis from which it failed to recover for several years.[38] He went on to become head of the Welsh School in Cardiff,[39] remaining there until his death in 1942, and claiming to *'avoid slave-like devotion to a rigid set of principles'*.[40] He was editor for the revised 1939 edition of Lethaby's *Architecture*, and he appears

15. Gateway to the Siemens Department of Thomas Firth & Sons, designed by W.S. Purchon in 1918, and now relocated in Savile Street East: one of only two known extant works by the school's first lecturer in the Sheffield area.

briefly in *The Architectural Review* of February 1923 writing a critique of the newly finished Museum of Wales by Smith and Brewer. A warm letter to the RIBA Journal following the publication of Gibbs's obituary in 1935 shows that Purchon had not forgotten his former patron.[41]

The Shaky Twenties
Purchon's resignation left a vacuum and the university threatened closure. A move into the College of Art was considered. Then Radford Smith was appointed as the new lecturer at £500 p.a. and the rule about practice was slightly relaxed allowing works valued at up to £4000, but also stipulating that if the lecturer resigned, he should not practise within 30 miles of Sheffield during the next three years. Vice-Chancellor Hadow opened the 1921 end-of-year exhibition to positive press reviews, and a prize was given for best sketchbook to Monica Davies, who became the first woman member of the Sheffield Society of Architects. The course descriptions at this stage had been rewritten in a concise and efficient manner, but with no mention of any design component in the first year, while in the second:

Designs based on historical periods are worked out according to the principles of Composition given in Lectures. These designs consist at first only of the elements of buildings; later, if the student shows ability, he may be permitted to proceed to the design of a complete building. [42]

Smith left after only two years and C.D. Carus-Wilson, architect of the Sheffield war memorial at Barker's Pool,[43] took over, but he stayed only a year.[44] Then St John Harrison was appointed for one year only at £400 p.a.. Herbert Leighton was still present as part-time assistant lecturer, and when in 1926 the library was reported to be in a neglected state, he was given the job of reordering it. Wigfull and Paterson were still contributing evening courses, but the school was failing to recruit new students, and by 1926 it had only four in comparison with an average of 45 students for schools outside London.[45] The Society of Architects supported the school through this difficult period and Gibbs, still personally involved, even guaranteed £500. But for three years running, from 1925-27, the University Calendar warned that the courses were *'purely provisional and liable to be amended or cancelled without further notice.'* It was evident that the school would die if not set upon a firmer footing.[46]

16. Conservatory extension to the house Claremont in Matlock, probably by W.S. Purchon who worked on the house.

17. (below) War memorial at Barker's Pool, Sheffield, 1924-25 by C.D. Carus-Wilson, lecturer in the school for a single year.

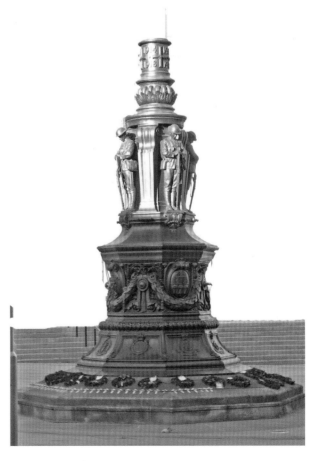

18. Stephen Welsh (photo courtesy of the Welsh family)
19. (below) A second year study of 'Greek Details' chosen for publication in the 1928 prospectus.

20. (above opposite) The school in its first home: the galleried tower room in Firth Court.

21, 22. (below opposite) Two more second year studies printed in the prospectus, following Classical and Gothic themes respectively.

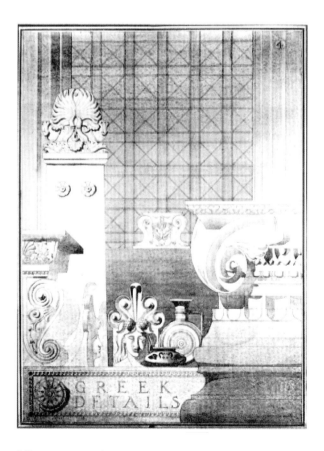

Stephen Welsh and Liverpool

The University at last took matters in hand, reorganising the school's studio room to expand its capacity from 18 drawing places to 28, and issuing a new prospectus to attract students, explicitly including women and naming as tutor for women students Dorothy Bennett. The main change, though, was to appoint a new young lecturer of energy and talent, Stephen Welsh. Still subsidising the school to the tune of £80 p.a., the Society finally relented on their restriction of the lecturer's right to practise,[47] but their fears in the end proved groundless, for despite a long and successful academic career, and despite becoming the first Professor of Architecture in 1948, Welsh in the end built little (primarily the Student Union).[48] Most of his energy went into the school.

Born in Forfar, Scotland, in 1892, Welsh was the son of a woodwork teacher. He left school early to work in architects' offices in Forfar and Glasgow before serving in Royal Engineers in the First World War. He was wounded in 1918 but recovered to join the Liverpool School of Architecture where he excelled, and which left its mark on him.[49] The Liverpool school had been founded in 1895, with a professor from its inception and more than 30 students by the turn of the century, achieving the first RIBA recognised courses in Britain.[50] It was led from 1904-1933 by Charles Reilly, a key figure in architectural education and the main champion of the French Beaux Arts system. In the RIBA Board of Education of 1911, there had been a significant split between Reilly and W.R. Lethaby, the champion of Arts and Crafts based education. Lethaby wanted architects to get their hands dirty, attending practical classes with bricklayers and plumbers, and doing engineering with the engineers, but the style of the work was to remain free, emerging somehow from this process. Reilly, in contrast, favoured 'The Grand Manner', spoke of the need for 'taste', and thought that the best way to achieve high design standards was to teach composition.[51] A book on the Liverpool school later summed up his ethos as *'strong abstract composition bearing informed cultural references'*, and a lecture given in Sheffield in 1909 also suggests a monumental tendency which is visible in some Liverpool student work:

We should try to give our buildings the appearance that they are not inhabited by ordinary mortals, but by a more leisured race with slightly bigger bodies and more refined perceptions than we ourselves possess.[52]

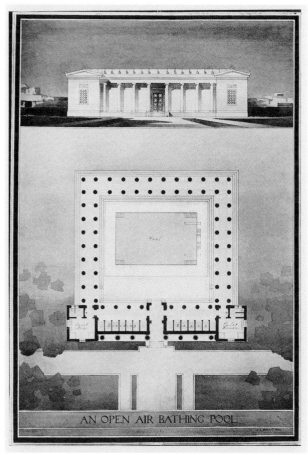

AN OPEN AIR BATHING POOL

A SOUTH PORCH TO A PARISH CHURCH

17

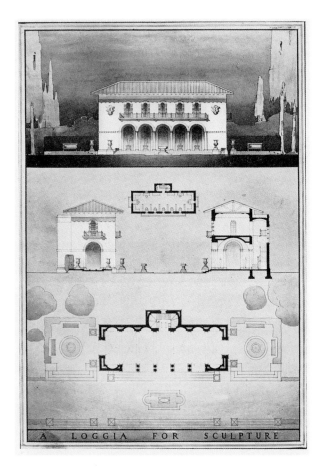

23, 24. Two more studies printed in the prospectus: above a fourth year Loggia for Sculpture, an 'exercise in proportion and detail', below a third year Tea-house.

By 1924 and the publication of his book *Some Architectural Problems of Today*, Reilly was in no doubt of his magisterial role as a leading guardian of public taste and promoter of aesthetic planning control. He comes across as a stylist, well confirmed in his classical prejudices, harping on about the virtues of the eighteenth century and reliance on the orders. The emphasis is on the façade and good civic manners, and the paradigm of architectural good taste is London's Somerset House. Lutyens and Burnet are current heroes, and American bank buildings are leading the way, while Norman Shaw, Ruskin, and the Gothic Revival are vilified. Arts and Crafts architecture should be left to the countryside and shows *'excessive individualism'*.[53]

The Liverpool school produced an average of four Rome scholars per year, Welsh being one of them in 1922.[54] Both Edwin Lutyens and Giles Gilbert Scott accepted honorary doctorates from Liverpool in the 1920s, and Maxwell Fry, William Holford, and William Crabtree (architect of that key modernist work the Peter Jones Department Store) were among its graduates at that time. A book about the school published in 1932 described Reilly's approach as 'Modernism with ancestry'.[55] Stephen Welsh had returned to teach there after graduating, and his Rome Scholarship drawings exhibited in Sheffield in 1923 were perhaps the initial point of contact. He officially took up his new post at Sheffield in October 1928, setting out his stall in the prospectus for 1928-9. It opens by describing the growth of architectural schools, still feeling a need to defend them against the pupilage system, perhaps in reaction to a last-ditch attempt to retain it at the RIBA conference on architectural education of 1924.[56] Welsh claimed that:

No private office, however extensive its work, can provide the student with a sufficiently wide outlook... In giving up [the pupilage system] and looking to Schools of Architecture, where students are entirely engaged on their own problems and daily competing one against the other, the architectural profession... is only following the practice of other countries... such as France and America.[57]

Modestly, Welsh concedes that *'the method of teaching is based on the general lines of the important architectural teaching centres'*, (read Liverpool) and then he gets into details of the curriculum. First year studio work begins with *'the classic orders... studied and drawn with*

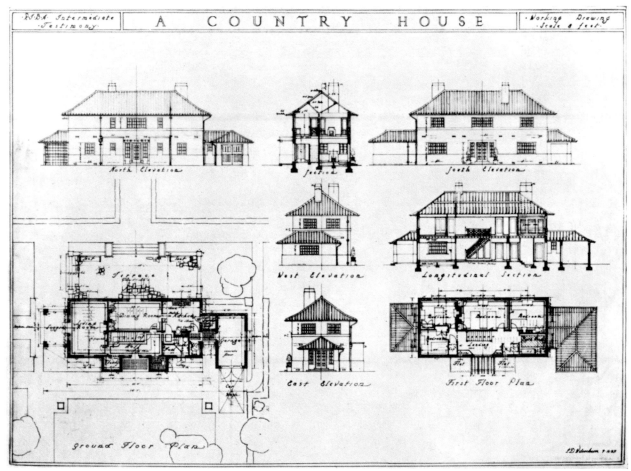

25. Drawings for a country house included in the prospectus as 'working drawings suitable for the RIBA Intermediate Testimonies of Study'.

special reference to their application in design'. Construction studies, descriptive geometry, presentation techniques and 'freehand drawing from the cast' are also involved, while 'the historical side' is pursued through lectures. In the second year *'design and construction are based on historical styles to establish a "standard of values"... and good proportion.'* The designs are taken further into construction studies and working drawings. History lectures continue. The third year student is finally allowed to *'design according to his own imagination'* and questions about the planning and grouping of buildings are engaged, as well as the pursuit of working drawings to contract level. There are studies of composition and materials, and studio work on furniture and decoration. In fourth and fifth years there may be specialisation in design or construction: *'In design stress is laid on logical planning as the basis of good architecture and the problems given are large and complex.'* After summarising the course as a whole, Welsh stresses the *'sketching and measuring of existing buildings of recognised interest and quality'* leading to the submission of a special set of measured drawings for the third year examination.[58]

Student Work from the 1920s

Eight carefully chosen drawings from earlier years reveal the spirit of the time. Dating back as far as 1920, they were presented on four plates at the end of the prospectus. The first shows first and second-year drawings of a 'Roman Corinthian Order' and 'Greek Details' including an Ionic capital. The second is shared between a second year gatehouse design 'Based on Gothic Elements' and a third year study for 'An Open-air Bathing Pool' treated as a classical atrium. The third plate sets a third year working drawing of 'A Country House' with plans, sections and elevations alongside a hexagonal 'Tea House in a Public Park'. The fourth combines a fourth year study for a 'Loggia for Sculpture' in a round-arched classical mode with a fifth year study for 'A Covered Bridge' in the classical manner. This correctly detailed extravaganza might easily have graced the drive of Castle Howard or some equally bombastic country house, and could have been built with minor adjustments at almost any time since the 17th century. The pre-modern style was of course to be expected in 1928, but the drawings reveal many other things that have changed in 80 years

19

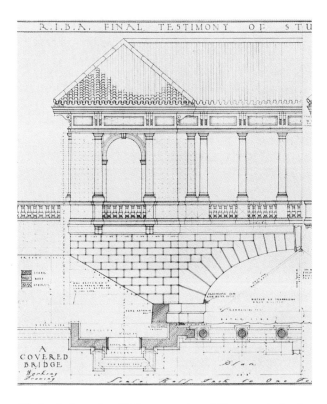

A
COVERED
BRIDGE
Working
Drawing
Scale Full Inch to One Foo

26. Again from the 1928 prospectus. Fifth year study of a covered bridge, captioned as 'Working drawing suitable for the RIBA Final Testimonies of Study'.

of architectural education. Perhaps most striking is the emphasis on drawing as a skill and as a finished product, on cartridge paper in pencil or ink with coloured wash. This encouraged a sense of completeness in the projected architecture and was impressive both for efficient presentation on a single sheet and for the way the building is cut off from context of any kind. While the buildings cannot be criticised as 'objects' in quite the same way as later Modernist ones, they do sit neatly on their pages, symmetrical and replete in their interlocking systems of axes, with all sense of neighbourliness missing from the discussion. Impressive for a modern audience also is the confident emphasis on drawing classical orders, casts of details, and approved canonical buildings. This procedure almost automatically combined skill in the art of representation with a clear definition of what constituted good architecture. Supported by books like Banister Fletcher,[59] this perpetuated a forceful view of stylistic correctness.

Welsh was evidently obliged to choose examples for his prospectus from work already done at the school before he took over, and was hardly in a position to challenge the established standards of measured drawing or reference to classical models. Nonetheless, in his report to the Sheffield Society of Architects he went out of his way to emphasise a more liberal attitude:

While the method of training seeks to familiarise the student with the good work of all periods and its lessons, no attempt is made to confine him, in his original work, to any particular 'manner' or phase of architecture. The school endeavours, rather, to develop the student's capacity for logical thought and characterisation in the solution of modern architectural problems.[60]

Welsh put his back into it, and he remained a commanding presence. By May 1929 he was demanding more money for assistance and for books and slides, and he got it. Student numbers picked up, so that by 1931 the grant from the Sheffield Society of Architects could be reduced from £80 to £50. The school's reputation also started to improve. In 1929 a Sheffield student, F. W. Wright, won an RIBA scholarship, and in 1930 Welsh initiated a junior section of the Society of Architects for students to join. In 1932 he 'modernised' the library, expelling and selling off what he perceived as useless books, and in December 1933 he achieved exemption for the school from the RIBA finals.[61] In 1936 the Society initiated its Rome Prize, and J.M.M. Jenkinson – son of the John Mansell Jenkinson who had taught in the early years – gained the first award. Even so, the school remained small by modern standards, never exceeding 50 students in total before 1940, while medicine at Sheffield already had more than 200.[62] It was also largely local in its provision, reflected in the recurrent names of the Sheffield architectural dynasties. The 1928-29 prospectus reported that *'students serve articles in Sheffield, Chesterfield, Doncaster, Rotherham and Barnsley'*.

Student work of the 1930s: Daykin

A witness of those years is Alec Daykin, student in the school from 1933-39 who returned after war duties and brief practice to become a member of staff in 1947, remaining until his retirement in 1989. During his years as a lecturer he enjoyed some additional reputation as a theatre set designer, and made the sets for the masque performed during the Queen's Jubilee visit of October 1954 to a script by William Empson.[63] Later he designed the conversion of the Drama Studio. Daykin also served as site architect for a series of archaeological digs with Colin Renfrew. He has given the school the surviving work from his student time, a series of 36 presentation drawings which show the range and type of projects undertaken.[64] They increase in size and complexity through the course, from a 'Dovecote' and a 'Lakeside Pavilion' in second year to a 'Repertory Theatre' in fourth and a 'Dental School' in fifth. The compulsory learning of orders and stylistic details in first year was followed up with frequent returns to Mediterranean themes, with a Museum in Greece in second year, perspectives of Italian and Egyptian scenes, and the design of a porch for an existing Italian church in fourth, a project requiring detailed knowledge of precedent and advanced compositional skill. Modernism breaks through in a third year seaside café, with flat roofs and portholes in the manner of Emberton, and more weakly in a fifth year Furniture Store with Mendelsohnian glazing at ground floor, but these were stylistic experiments unsupported by modernist tectonics. Daykin claims that Welsh had no time for Le Corbusier, and the underlying manner of his pupils reflected Welsh's own restrained Neo-Georgian, powerfully exemplified by his Student Union Building of 1936 (fig 36, p 25).[65] Daykin's most confident and detailed drawings, such as his 'Half inch Details of a Branch Bank' show that this lesson was well learned. With such drawings laboured over in the studio day after day, the end of year shows must have been impressive, demonstrating to visitors perhaps more clearly than today precisely the skills that the architect offered. Attractively turned out in plan, section, elevation, and perspective, the buildings were neat, complete, and apparently buildable. Detailing concentrated on visible elements, assuming that builders could decide what went on underneath the plaster. Stylistic features were developed with consistency and clarity. Planning was relatively unadventurous, following the axial Beaux Arts method which was not well-geared to asymmetry. Sites were often imaginary, and written programmes from the late 1940s – the earliest found – are consistently accompanied by small site plans concocted by Professor Welsh showing only things in the immediate vicinity, and only in plan. Formal gardens would be drawn in delicate shades of green to complement the buildings, but even when difficult urban situations were tackled, neighbouring structures hardly intruded into the elevations. Some designs were executed against the clock in the Beaux Arts manner, and Daykin retained a demonstration design for a royal box completed in front of his students in just two hours. Buildings were technically simpler, less information was required, but the drawing skill was greater, reinforced by measured surveys of existing buildings that honed visual perception as well as graphic skill.

27. Drawings from the student portfolio of Alec Daykin: A dovecote, second year, 1936/37.

28. (below) A lakeside pavilion, second year, 1936/37: almost modernist, with a ghost of an entablature.

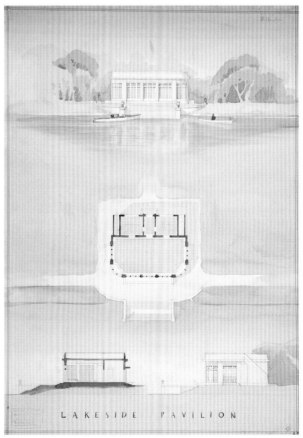

MUSEUM IN GREECE.

29. Drawings from the student portfolio of Alec Daykin: 'Museum in Greece', second year, 1936/37, classical perform-ance on an ideal site.

30. (below left) Untitled tempietto/chapel with figures, elevation in colour wash, third year, 1937-8.

31. (below right) 'An Italian Stair', perspective, fourth year, 1938/39.

32. (opposite) 'A Porch to an Italian Church', design project, fourth year, 1938-9.

A PORCH
TO AN ITALIAN
CHURCH.
SKETCH DESIGN

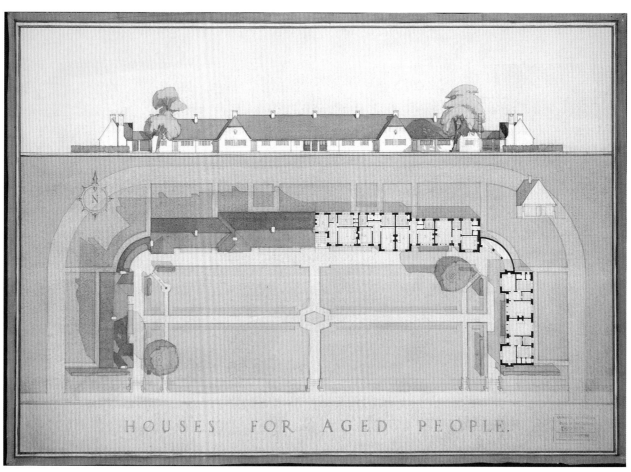

HOUSES FOR AGED PEOPLE.

More drawings from the student portfolio of Alec Daykin.
33. (above) 'Houses for Aged People', a single drawing of plan and elevation to show the concept and organisation, third year 1937/38.

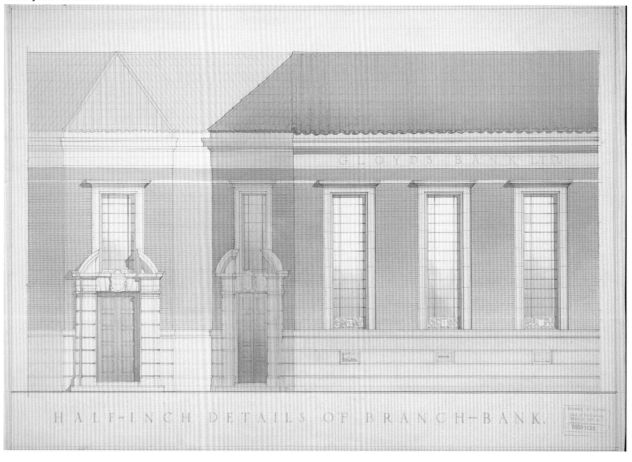

HALF-INCH DETAILS OF BRANCH-BANK.

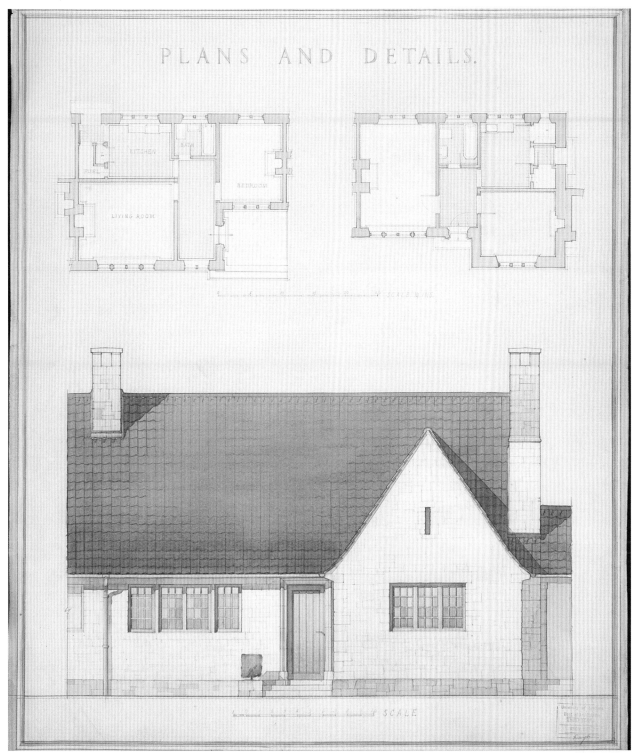

PLANS AND DETAILS.

34. (opposite) 'Half inch Details of Branch Bank', elevations in colour wash, third year 1937-38. Typically for the time, these drawings concentrate on the visible detail and surfaces rather than the underlying construction.

35. (above) 'Plans and Details' (of the Houses for Aged People seen opposite), third year, 1937-8. Moving to a larger scale, these drawings show both the detailed planning and the visible apects of construction.

36. (right) Stephen Welsh, University of Sheffield Student's Union 1936, Welsh's most important commission from the university and the most locally prominent example of his work.

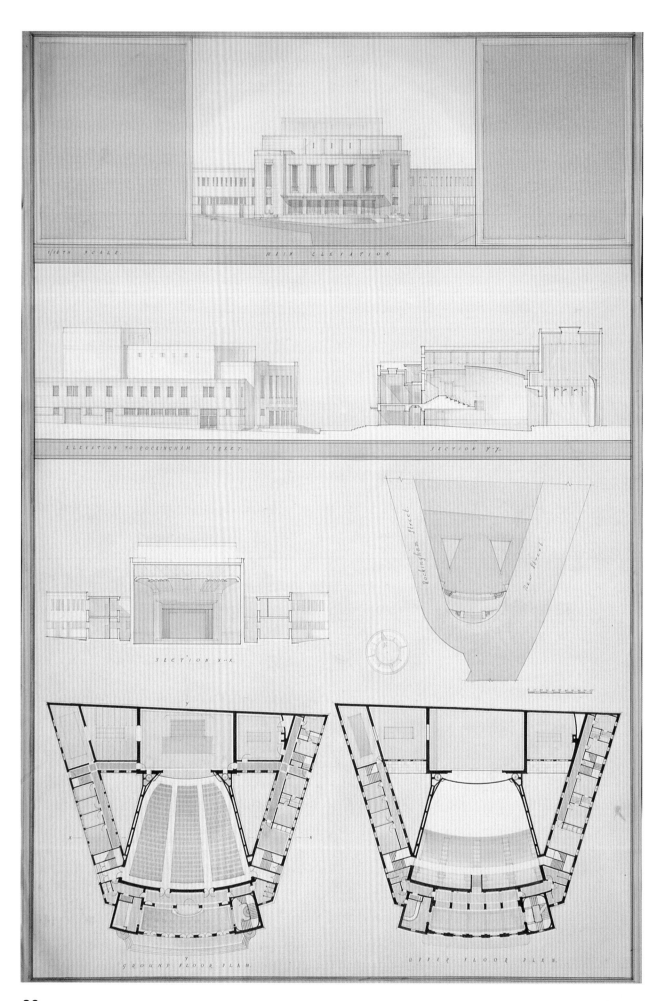

1/16TH SCALE.   MAIN ELEVATION.

ELEVATION TO ROCKINGHAM STREET.   SECTION Y-Y.

SECTION X-X.

GROUND FLOOR PLAN.   UPPER FLOOR PLAN.

26

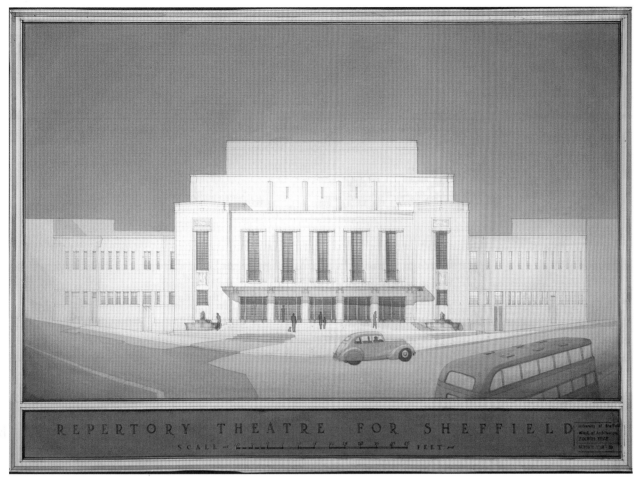

REPERTORY THEATRE FOR SHEFFIELD

SCALE — ... — FEET —

More drawings from the student portfolio of Alec Daykin.

37. (opposite) 'Repertory Theatre for Sheffield', at corner of Rockingham St and New St, fourth year, 1938/39.

38. (above) 'Repertory Theatre for Sheffield, front elevation, fourth year, 1938/39.

39. (below left) 'A Furniture Store', fifth year, 1939-40; modernist with Mendelsohnian shop windows.

40. (below right) 'A Seaside Café-Restaurant', perspective' third year, undated. A modernist white design with flat roofs and portholes in the Emberton manner.

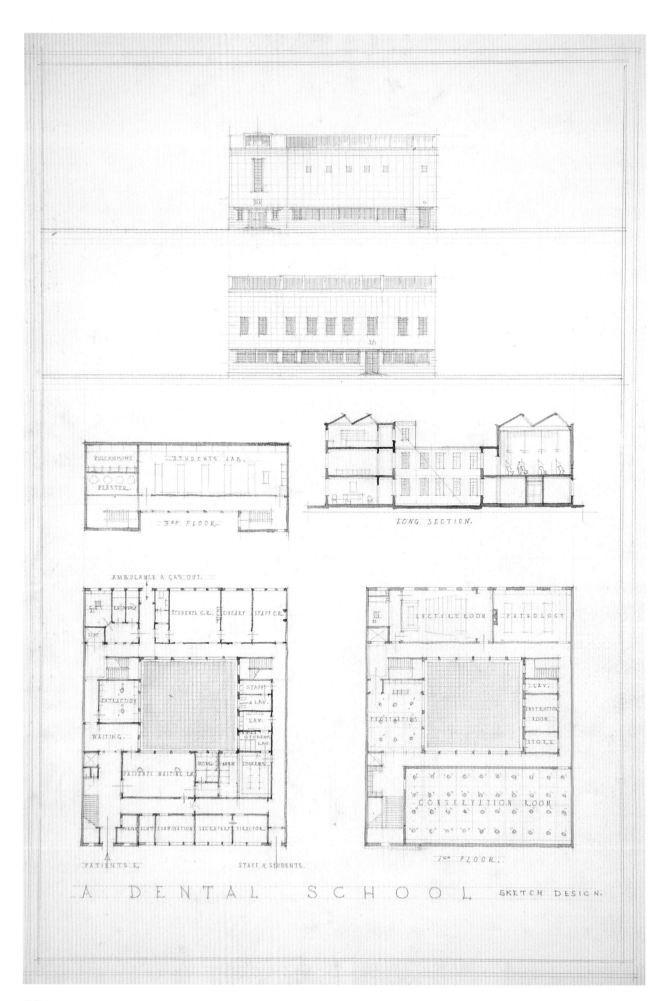

VULCANISING STUDENTS LAB.

PLASTER.

3RD. FLOOR.

LONG SECTION.

AMBULANCE & GAS OUT.

C.R. LECTURE STUDENTS C.R. LIBRARY STAFF C.R.

LIFT

EXTRACTION STAFF & LAV.

LAV.

WAITING. STUDENT LAV.

WOMAN MAN LOCKERS

PATIENTS WAITING RM

EXAMINATION SECRETARY DIRECTOR

PATIENTS E. STAFF & STUDENTS.

LECTURE ROOM PATHOLOGY

LAV.

PROSTHETICS INSTRUCTION ROOM

STORE

CONSERVATION ROOM

7TH FLOOR.

A DENTAL SCHOOL SKETCH DESIGN.

28

Post-war Changes

The University Calendar of 1939 lists Stephen Welsh as lecturer and head of department, with two full time teaching assistants, two drawing instructors, and two further staff teaching construction, the senior of these being the early ex-student Herbert Leighton. Additional 'short courses' were provided in strength of materials, the properties of clay and glass, surveying, acoustics, and lighting. In 1938-39 and 1939-40, ten students passed through the intermediate examination each year, seven and eight through the final. Of this total of 35, five were women (14%). The total student body in architecture was 40 in 1938, 46 in 1940,[66] which in relation to the full-time staff of seven meant a staff/student ratio of 1:6.5. After 1945, the bulge of returning soldiers combined with a post-war expansion of education was strongly felt in Sheffield, and student numbers in architecture had risen to 174 by 1950.[67] There was a corresponding increase in staff: by 1947 Welsh's full-time teachers (now listed as lecturers) had risen from two to six (in addition to the four in drawing and construction), and when he was promoted to the first chair of architecture the following year, there were eight. The staff/student ratio in 1950 works out at 1:12.5. This staffing level remained more or less constant until Professor Welsh's retirement in 1957. The expansion also triggered a change of accommodation. Since the tower room in Firth Court offered no further possibilities for expansion, the school moved out into the redundant Sunday school in Shearwood Road, next to the church used today as the University's Drama Studio. This warren of small rooms grouped around a couple of small halls was not given to architecture alone, but was shared at first with forensic medicine, extramural studies, and part of geography, though in 1954 more space was leased from the church for architecture.[68] The architecture library was in the basement. Curiously, as its main teaching space it offered again a toplit studio surrounded by a gallery, from which Professor Welsh could survey his charges and bark instructions.[69]

Student work of the early 1950s

The thesis project of David Allford, later to become the leading second generation partner in YRM (Yorke, Rosenberg and Mardall), gives a glimpse of the progressive side of work done in the school during the immediate post-war years (see following spread). Allford had grown up in Sheffield and chose the suitably social theme of industrial relations. It was a large and complex building, ideal for showing the student's prowess

41. (opposite) Student project for a dental school by Alec Daykin, fifth year, 1939-40.

42. (above) Aerial photograph of the school's second home: the Sunday school complex in Shearwood Road.

43. (below) The new architecture studio in the former Sunday school, again a galleried space.

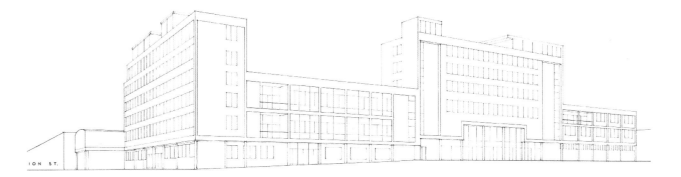

ION ST.

Final Year thesis project by David Allford, 1952, for an 'Industrial Relations Centre' in Sheffield, set between West Street and Division Street.

44. (above) Perspective.
45. (below) Ground and First Floor Plans.

46. (opposite top) Elevations.
47. (opposite bottom) Upper plans.

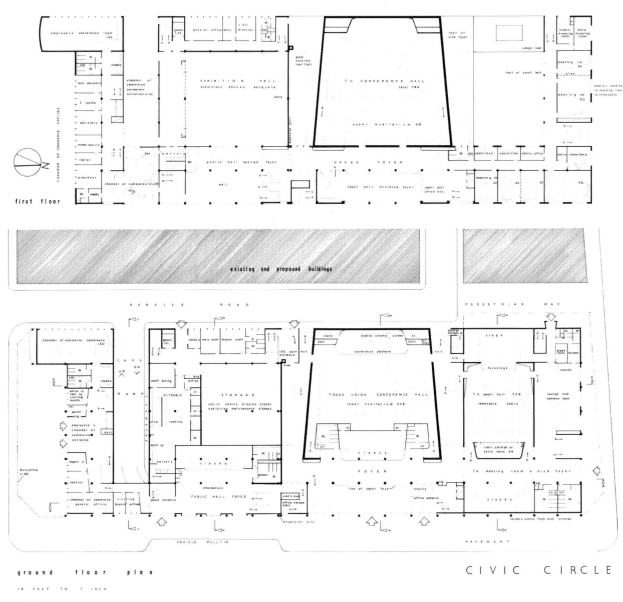

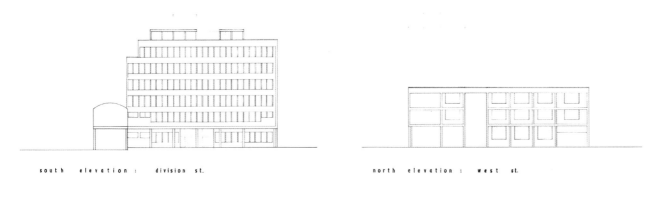

south elevation : division st.

north elevation : west st.

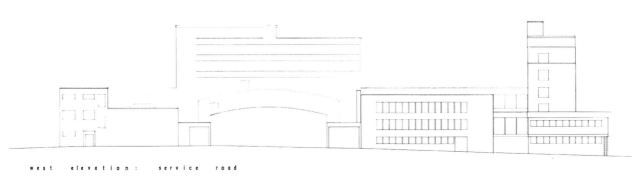

west elevation : service road

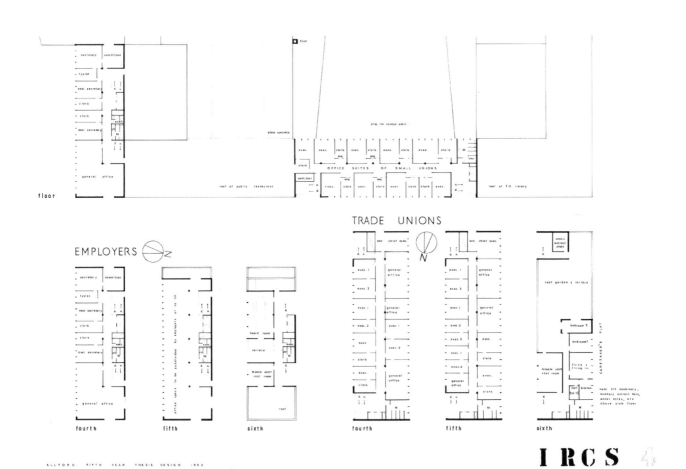

EMPLOYERS

TRADE UNIONS

floor

fourth   fifth   sixth

fourth   fifth   sixth

ALLFORD   FIFTH   YEAR   THESIS   DESIGN   1952

I R C S

INDUSTRIAL RELATIONS CENTRE SHEFFIELD

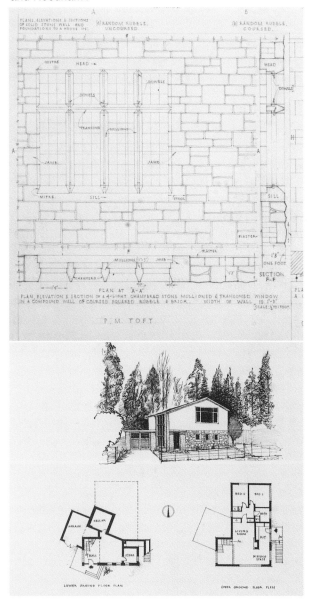

"THE ESSENTIAL QUALITIES OF GOOD LETTERING ARE LEGIBILITY, BEAUTY AND CHARACTER."

P.M.TOFT. FIRST YEAR. OCT.54.

Drawings from the student portfolio of Philip Toft.
48. Lettering study, first year, 1954.

49. (below) Stonework details, part of 'Construction sheet no. 1', first year, 1954.

50. (bottom) Second year precedent study, December 1955, redrawn plan and constructed perspective of 'House at Dundee designed by Gauldie, Hardie, Wright and Needham'.

in solving the organisational issues, and displaying an interest typical of the time in articulating the various functions in separate blocks, then letting the rationality of the construction dominate. It was also a typically socialist project in that it gave the trades unions priority over the employers by setting them in the main facade over the conference hall. The very complete set of drawings in sober black and white further reflects the modernist theme.

Student work lower down the school is well reflected by the portfolio of Philip Toft, who later worked for the city architect and then in private practice. It gives a glimpse of the mid 1950s, the final years of Stephen Welsh's reign. Technical teaching began in first year with carefully drawn studies of brick bonding and the detailing of different kinds of stonework, and this kind of traditional construction was played out in projects like the second year doctor's house of 1955 (opposite), set in a small village by the church and with stone-mullioned windows and leaded lights. The plain door to the left of the garage is for patients visiting the surgery, while the doctor and his family take the grander Tudor porched door to the right. Professor Welsh still clung to his Beaux Arts heritage by setting classical sketch projects like 'A Prison Gate' (fig 53) or 'A Well House' (fig 54), and a project for 'An Italian Garden' on an imaginary site persisted in third year, but modernism broke through from time to time. A flat roofed rowing club (fig 55) appears in second year, a concrete water tower in third, then in fourth year a fully horizontal and asymmetrical 'Directors' offices for a firm of aircraft constructors' (fig 56). Modernist buildings were also studied as precedents, and by a strange coincidence Toft made study drawings of a house by Gauldie, Hardie, Wright and Needham (below left), the practice of the next professor who was to arrive in Sheffield two years later. Design projects were served up in beautiful perspectives in watercolour wash, a high standard being achieved quite early, and there was stringent instruction in lettering in first year, which in Toft's case led to a fruitful sideline as a letterer in later life. One of the most impressive items in Toft's portfolio is a huge and delicate measured drawing of the façade of Senate House in Cambridge (overleaf, p 35) executed in the summer between first year and second. It involved a four-day visit to the city, scrambling around on the building with measuring tapes and ladders. The preparatory sketches noting details and dimensions in many separate drawings reveal the enormous amount of labour that went into these productions.

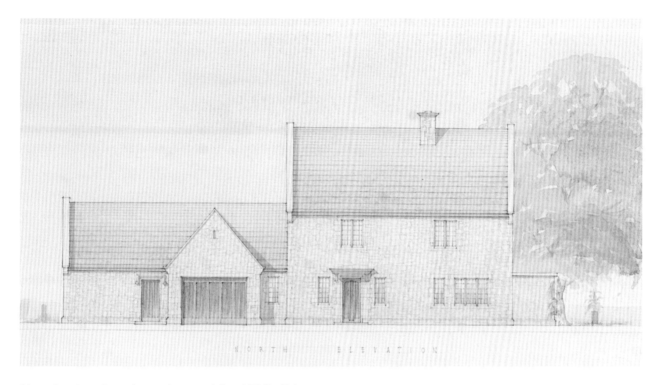

More drawings from the student portfolio of Philip Toft.
51. North elevation of 'House for a Doctor' second year, 1955/56. The stone mullioned and transomed windows, appropriate for a pillar of the community in a country village, are based on the technology displayed in the drawing opposite. The doctor has a car and a prominent garage.

52. (below) Plans and perspective of 'House for a Doctor', second year, 1955/56. The perspective suggests the traditional English village setting with a church tower behind, but the site plans were usually of imaginary places drawn in plan in a few lines by the professor.

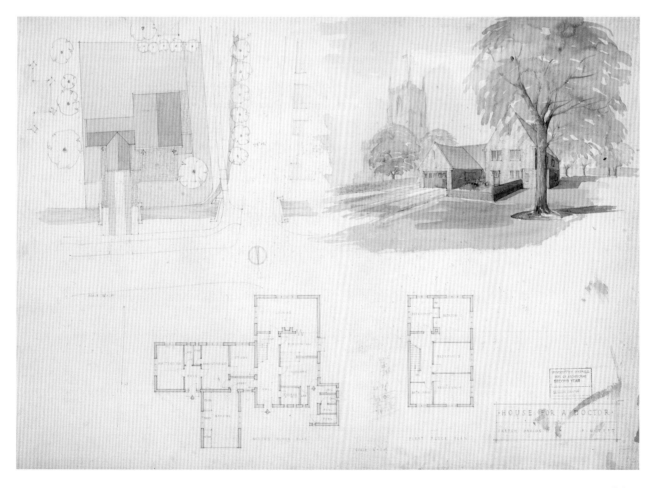

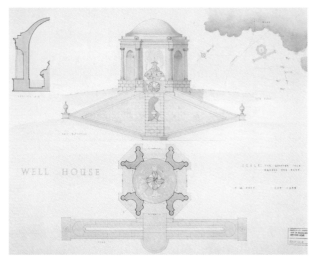

More drawings from the student portfolio of Philip Toft.
53. (left) Design for 'A Prison Gate', a second year exercise dated November 1955.

54. (above) Design for 'A Well House' also second year.

55. (below) Perspective of 'A Small Rowing Club', second year design programme, dated April 1956.

56. (bottom) North elevation of 'Directors' Offices for a Firm of Aircraft Constructors', third year design programme 1956-57.

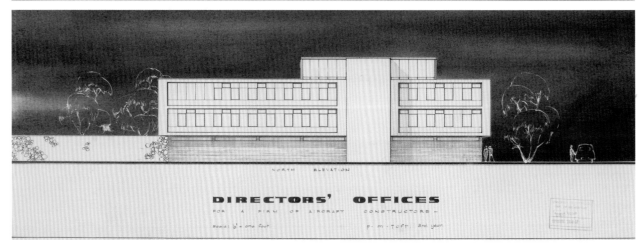

57. Final presentation drawing of The Senate House, Cambridge, by Philip Toft: the measured drawing submitted for his degree, executed at a scale of 1/3rd inch to one foot.

58. (below) Detail of the same drawing showing a capital.
59. (below right) Sketches recording measured dimensions, dated July 1955.

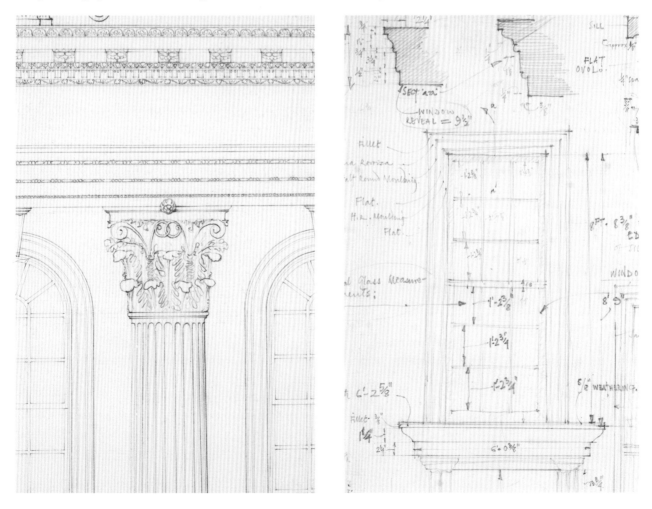

60. Professor John Needham, head of school from 1957-1973.

61. (below) John Needham showing work at the school to Kenzo Tange during a visit to the school of 1970 when Tange received an honourary doctorate. In the background is John Page.

62. (opposite top) Professor John Page, head of the newly founded department of Building Science, 1960.

63. (opposite middle) Building science students making a windflow test, 1968.

64. (opposite bottom) Geoffrey Tattersall (left) testing the effect of vibration on the consolidation of concrete.

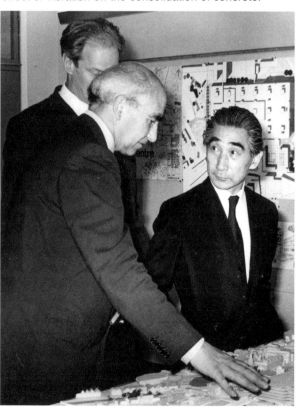

Needham, Page and Building Science

Welsh had been head of school for 29 years and professor for nine when he retired in 1957. The next professor and head for 14 years, John Needham (1909-1990), was a quieter, less colourful character. Born in Yorkshire and trained at Leeds, he had moved to Dundee in 1938 to take up the headship of the School of Architecture at the College of Art, and had been appointed to the RIBA Board of Education in 1940. In 1950 he became a partner in the practice Gauldie Hardie Wright and Needham, designers of the Guardian Royal Exchange building, Dundee, of 1955, but he continued to head the Dundee school. His move to Sheffield caused him almost to drop out of practice, but in the mid 1960s he designed a church in Sheffield, St Luke's Lodge Moor, assisted by a future head, Kenneth Murta.[70] He also played a role in the city's conservation, becoming the Sheffield Society of Architects' member of the Civic Society.[71]

Needham's strength seems to have lain in his social and administrative skills, quietly accomplishing much for the school by presiding over an enormous expansion including the creation of the Faculty of Architectural Studies. He was astute in his selection of staff, three of whom went on to become heads at other schools of architecture.[72] The students often found him remote, but when John Allan and three other undergraduates bravely complained to his famously fierce secretary, Maisie Crawford, that they had not seen enough of their prof and wanted to invite him for a drink, the message got through. He complied with their request and spent a cordial evening with them, impressed by their initiative.[73]

One effect of Needham's headship was that the Beaux Arts emphasis on measured drawing and watercolour wash technique, by then rather old-fashioned, was relaxed. The modernist ethos which had taken over required a crisp clarity of presentation, and the dissemination of exemplary works in books and journals favoured hard line drawings, everything in monochrome. Drawings in practice were now geared to dye-line printing, which allowed the multiple copies necessary both for consultation and site work, and put a premium on clarity, switching the medium to ink and tracing paper. This change in technique is evident in student work of the period and reflected in the fact that under Needham drawing was subsumed into the general studio tuition instead of being the province of the named specialists who at one time under Welsh had constituted almost a third of the staffing.[74]

Needham's time also brought an increased emphasis on the technical side. Developments in technology and materials, the need for larger, deeper, more heavily serviced buildings, and the modernist belief in the superiority and inevitability of mass-production, all meant an abandonment of old slow craft methods in favour of system building. Not only were architects obsessed with the new technological possibilities, but this ethos pervaded society, epitomised by Harold Wilson's 'white heat of technology' speech at the Labour Conference of 1963.[75] Science was exciting and progressive, and the RIBA's Oxford Conference on Architectural Education of 1958 had sought to realign the subject with the better-funded physical sciences, driving architecture departments out of art colleges into universities, and switching the A level entry requirement for students to physics and mathematics. At Cambridge Leslie Martin, Professor of Architecture since 1956 and presiding genius of the Oxford Conference, was setting up what became the Martin Centre for architectural research. Parallel moves in the drive towards objective science were made at the Bartlett (University College London) by Richard Llewellyn-Davies.

At Sheffield Stephen Welsh had already recognised the growing need for building science, and there had long been collaborations with technical departments in the university concerned with the properties of glass, clay and metals, but little had been done on the environmental side. Sensing a potential strength, the university set up a Department of Building Science in 1960, luring Cambridge-trained physicist John Page away from Liverpool to take up the headship and a new chair. His early career had included work on the Festival of Britain and a period at the nascent Building Research Station. He had also worked at the Nuffield Foundation under Llewellyn-Davies. He brought to Sheffield an expertise in relating buildings to climate, initiating several research programmes which involved physical measurement, including the construction of a wind tunnel. After the oil crisis of 1973, he initiated an interest group concerned with energy use in buildings which has continued until today in various forms, and as microcomputers were developed they were applied to climatic assessment. The Sheffield school gained a reputation for technical proficiency, and Page served on several national and international boards and committees, increasing the university's influence and reputation. He played a significant role locally in the creation of

65. First year students in the building science laboratory.

66. (below) Traffic noise measurements being made by Eric Stanley in the 19th floor of the Arts Tower.

the Faculty of Architectural Studies in 1965 of which he was twice Dean, and in the initiation of the two new departments that helped to constitute it, Town and Regional Planning and Landscape Architecture.[76]

Several students in the school in the 1960s and 1970s have spoken glowingly of the building science teaching, which seems to have become well-integrated with their projects, judging by the competence of their technical drawings. Anne Minors, who was in the school between 1973 and 1979, finished with a distinction, and is now an internationally renowned theatre consultant (see her thesis project, pages 58-59), remembered the enthusiastic teaching of John Page, and referred twice in our conversation to his influence, once in relation to the shadows cast by buildings and once in relation to the technical non-viability of flat roofs.[77] She also spoke warmly of Geoffrey Tattersall and his thorough studies of concrete, claiming it was he above all others who demonstrated the principle that one should research an issue thoroughly and get to the bottom of it. Tattersall was a leading figure nationally in the development of slump tests for concrete.

From Local to International
The Sheffield School had been started by local architects to serve local needs, but the expansion after 1945 brought students from a wider field, who on graduation returned to different parts of the country and across the world. There were African and Malaysian students as early as the 1950s, and Sheffield's first Malaysian architectural graduate, Ikmal Hisham Albakri (1930-2006), became principal of one of that country's leading practices, Kumpulan Akitek, which built the National Library and Putra World Trade Center as well as numerous hotels and large commercial buildings. He became the first president of the Malaysian Architectural Association (PAM) and a recipient of its Gold Medal, while also involved internationally in organisations such as the UIA. Towards the end of his life he was showered with honours including the title Dato (equivalent of a knighthood) and an honorary doctorate from Sheffield. The connection with Malaysia continued and there have since been many further Malaysian alumni.[78]

If before the war, the school's natural role had been to train architects largely for the city and locality, post-war commissions for large buildings in Sheffield were increasingly awarded to outside practices, often to firms in London or Manchester.

This had started with designs for buildings like the Town Hall of 1890-97 and the City Hall of 1928-32, both awarded to outsiders through competitions, but by the post-war years even humdrum commercial buildings were being designed by outside practices. No private practice in Sheffield became renowned enough to counterbalance this loss by building significantly elsewhere, but fame did accrue to the local authority office of City Architect Lewis Womersley (in post 1953-63). It built many schools and other social buildings that were highly thought of at the time,[79] but its greatest triumph lay in housing work of world importance. Because of its armaments production, Sheffield had been heavily bombed, becoming a deserving site for public investment and experiment spurred on by a left-wing council. For young architects in the 1950s the prospect of a career in a local government office was highly attractive, combining job security with a real sense of social service and a chance to work on large and progressive projects. These pioneers of modernism relished engaging with the new technologies of system building as well as joining a brotherhood of teamwork as idealised by Walter Gropius. Park Hill (1955-61) has remained the figurehead, long considered the prime example nationally of slab-block housing with streets in the air, and celebrated as a key work of 'The New Brutalism'.[80] It was designed by Jack Lynn and Ivor Smith, both of whom taught part-time in the school of architecture. Half a century later, following the era of *'private affluence and public squalor'*,[81] the dismantling of local government by Margaret Thatcher and the accompanying move towards privatisation, it has become hard to empathise with the ideal of welfare state service that then prevailed, or to understand the pride felt by the first tenants of Park Hill on abandoning their slums for new flats.

The spate of progressive public work in Sheffield brought influential publications like a whole special issue of *Architectural Design* in September 1961,[82] and there was even a short-lived local journal modelled on national ones like *The Architectural Review* and *Architectural Design* called *Design in Sheffield*.[83] In 1963 the RIBA's annual conference was held in the city, with Lewis Womersley and the Sheffield Society of Architects acting as host.[84] Professor Needham was on the committee and the university provided support. There was a dinner in the Cutlers' Hall, a garden party at Chatsworth, numerous visits to recent local buildings, and even helicopter flights over the city. The theme of the conference was 'The Architect and Productivity', reflecting a period of boom and technological

67. Cover of the special issue of *Architectural Design* dedicated to Sheffield, September 1961.

68. (below) Park Hill, the housing by the City Architect's Department, as displayed in simplified drawings in the same *Architectural Design* issue.

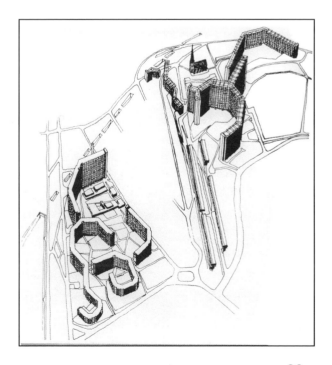

39

69. Sculpture by first year architecture student Andrew Armitage on Western Bank with University House behind, 1963.

70. (below) Perspective of a preliminary version of the Arts Tower as seen from the east.

change, but there were also growing fears about excessive repetition and loss of quality: as RIBA President Robert Matthew put it: *'Productivity which increases the output of ugliness or gives an endless stale repetition of bad designs is not worth having'*.[85]

One of the most visited groups of new buildings during the RIBA's Sheffield conference was that of the university on Western Bank, and parts of the conference took place there. A competition had been held among first year students at the School of Architecture for a commemorative sculpture, and the winning design by Andrew Armitage was executed in stainless steel donated by Bryta Works and Firth Vickers. It stood 18 foot high on Western Bank, but was later removed and has since been lost.[86] Conference delegates were entertained at University House, one of the series of new buildings by the London firm Gollins Melvin and Ward (henceforth GMW), who had won the national competition for extending the university in 1953. GMW's university library, completed in 1959, was acclaimed by Nikolaus Pevsner as *'the best individual twentieth-century building in Sheffield'*.[87] Built as part of the same scheme were the Hicks Building, the Bursary, and the extension to the Chemistry Department. The Arts Tower, intended from the start to dominate the whole composition, was still under construction in 1963, but it was already destined to be the new home of the School of Architecture.

Move into the Arts Tower
As Professor of Architecture, Stephen Welsh had played a crucial role in the setting up of the competition of 1952-3, acting as a go-between with the RIBA, meeting its president, and helping to define the conditions.[88] The expert judges were Percy Thomas and F.R.S. Yorke, author of *The Modern House* and partner in Yorke, Rosenberg and Mardall.[89] There were 99 entries, and three prizes were awarded: the first to GMW, and the other two to local firms: Mansell Jenkinson and Cruickshank and Seward. The now famous designs by James Stirling and Allison and Peter Smithson went completely unnoticed.[90] GMW's scheme (opposite), heavily influenced by the American work of Ludwig Mies van der Rohe, was praised for its simplicity and uniformity. The avoidance of closed courts was welcomed as 'open and spacious', while the elevations were regarded as 'contemporary in character'.[91] The library stood in its final position overlooking Western Park, but the Arts Tower was initially sited

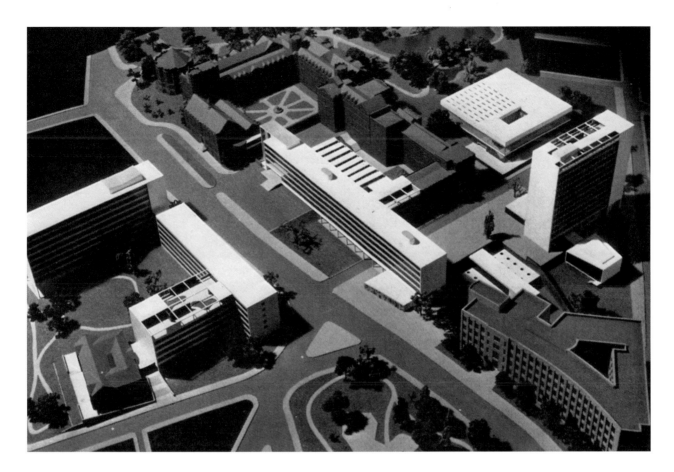

further to the east, its front looking across towards the library as the connection between them was considered important. It had only 13 storeys and architecture was accommodated elsewhere, part of an outer courtyard extending Firth Court where its studios could be appropriately daylit. Execution was phased, and requirements changed as the university expanded. Debates went on between the university and the architects about what should go where, and how much money could be spent. Doubts about a tall building were already voiced in 1956, when Professor Welsh presented alternative diagrams of the accommodation at five to seven storeys, but the committee chairman reassured his members that that there was *'no objection to a high building provided that the lift system is adequate'*.[92] The possibility of solar overheating was also raised, but the architects had been wedded from the start to their concept of a universal curtain wall, and single glazing with internal Venetian blinds were then the norm. The only negotiation on offer was the cill height. The comparative generosity and expense of the ground floor, mezzanine and great well, which are architecturally the making of the building, were surprisingly little challenged.

With the retirement of Professor Welsh in 1957, Professor Needham took over as architectural

71. Model of GMW's competition-winning masterplan for the university of 1953. The Arts Tower and library are to the right.

72. (below) GMW's competition winning site plan, showing the existing buildings in black and their proposed ones in white. Note the generous pedestrian plaza and the proposed link through to Western Park.

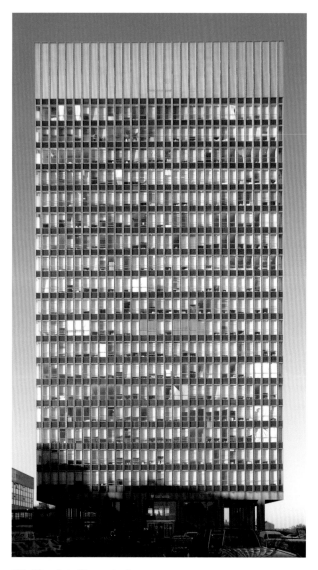

73. The Arts Tower today.

74. (below) The entrance steps, which were once flanked with ponds on either side

adviser, and was immediately invited by the Vice-Chancellor, Dr J. M. Whittaker – originally a mathematician – to share leadership of the planning sub-committee, but as a newcomer he could hardly argue with his boss. Far from giving him his head, Dr Whittaker became personally engaged with the project and took against the proposal, rejecting the 'slab block' as too anonymous, and wanting something that more obviously signalled 'university'. He even considered dismissing the architects, but was reassured by the charismatic Lewis Womersley. He fought hard in the committee for a cylindrical building and very nearly won, but the architects produced the trump card of greatly increased structural costs, so he backed down muttering regrets.[93]

The tower had been accepted, and in 1958 the committee agreed to cancel the proposed low-rise School of Architecture, adding the whole of its accommodation instead to the top of the Arts Tower. The building therefore rose to 20 storeys, and a promised extra lift to link the five top floors within architecture never materialised, presumably because of cost. The idea of the university owning the tallest building in the city flattered all, and the views from the school of architecture would show *'how town-planning was going on'*, but the relatively small plan area of the building also helped, for it made the logistics of site-planning and demolition much easier, and everything could be done with one crane. In the event, too, the Miesian concept of a flexible all-purpose building with standard spaces of a few basic sizes lent itself well to the chaotic process of assigning and reassigning spaces that took place between the initial concept and the inhabited building. The potential flexibility of the non-structural partitions has over 40 years proved useful, for changing floor-plans reveal how they been shifted around.[94]

Despite these advantages, the Vice-Chancellor's critical instincts in reacting against the Arts Tower's relative anonymity and lack of architectural rhetoric were not ill-founded, for it still reads as a mere office block, the presence of the large lecture theatres completely suppressed by sinking them in the ground. They form a base which from the start has served as a car park rather than the intended plaza, quickly losing the mitigation of decorative ponds to either side of the entrance due to the wind-driven spray which made them unworkable. But the building has had its friends. Nikolaus Pevsner backed the Arts Tower both in principle and in practice, even citing it in a radio broadcast as an exemplary piece of Functionalism in contrast with Stirling and Gowan's naughty Leicester Engineering Building, which he attacked as 'Expressionist'.[95] This argument later provoked great scorn from one of the users, Geoffrey Broadbent, who had lectured in the School of Architecture for two years before he moved on to the headship at Portsmouth. Looking back in 1980, he claimed that the Arts Tower could hardly be regarded as 'functional' because:

I was suffering from thoroughly inadequate vertical circulation - there were two 40 seater lecture rooms on the roof served by one 10 person lift - from solar heat gain (97°F in my room one day, with snow on the ground outside), glare, noise transmission through floors and partitions, a wind vortex at the base which sometimes made it impossible to enter the front door, and so on. How could Pevsner describe it as 'functional'. It was rectilinear in form and glass curtain-walled, it looked machine-made; so, for Pevsner it must be 'functional'.[96]

The Faculty of Architectural Studies

In 1965 Architecture and Building Science together took over the upper floors of the newly built tower, though the building was not officially 'opened' until 1966. The staff were happy, for the rehoused departments were generously equipped, space standards being luxurious by comparison with previous conditions at Shearwood Road. John Allan, who arrived as a student within months of the official opening, was probably exaggerating when he said he enjoyed *'better working conditions as a first year student than I've had ever since – including being director of my own company,'* but he was clearly impressed.[97]

Student numbers in Architecture were to be limited to 200, less than half of the number present today.[98] Professor Page's insistence that Architecture and Building Science were housed together paid off, and serious laboratory space was included. There had been discussions within the School of Architecture about sister departments and about forming a Faculty of Architectural Studies as early as 1963. There were two reasons to press for this independence: first the Faculty of Arts was too large and unwieldy, second, the BA Hons still required architectural students to take another arts subject, an arrangement persisting since the school's switch to arts in 1912, but which now seemed superfluous. The new faculty was duly created and first appears in the

75. The new architecture studios just prior to occupation.
76. (below left) J.R. James, first Professor of Town and Regional Planning.
77. (below right) Arnold Weddle, first Professor of Landscape Architecture.

University Calendar for the academic year 1965-6 with Professor Needham as Dean. The nascent Department of Town and Regional Planning then had just two lecturers, and not until three years later in 1968-9 was there a Landscape Architecture Department with a single lecturer in comparison with Town Planning's five.

In that same year, 1968-9, the two new departments were for the first time headed by professors. Town and Regional Planning was lucky to get John Richings James, who since 1961 had been Chief Planner in the Ministry of Housing and Local Government. Trained as a geographer, he had entered the civil service as a research officer at the Ministry of Town and Country Planning in

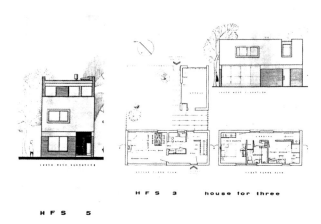

HFS 5

HFS 3   house for three

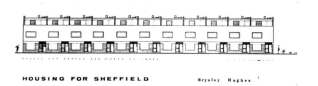

HOUSING FOR SHEFFIELD   Brynley Hughes

Three student projects from Architecture published in the 1965 first Faculty Prospectus.

78. Housing for Sheffield by Brynley Hughes, second year.

79. (below) Student Hostel by D. Fingland, third year.

80. (opposite) Art Gallery for Sheffield by T.M.Russell, thesis project.

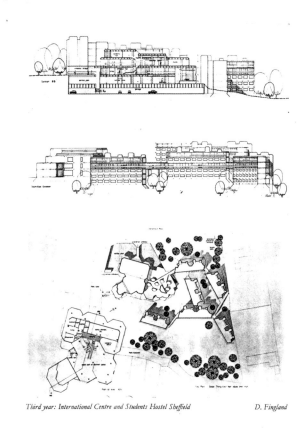

Third year: International Centre and Students Hostel Sheffield   *D. Fingland*

Newcastle in 1946, sorting out the problems of Peterlee and Aycliffe new towns before climbing the career ladder and turning his attention to larger scale development plans.[99] There was dismay in Whitehall when he left, but the new Sheffield department could hardly have hoped for a more distinguished head with better contacts or greater political skills. Even so, his large-scale strategic and political interests launched the department on a trajectory that steadily diverged from the local place-making concerns of architecture, failing to exploit the potential shared territory of urban design.

The first Professor of Landscape Architecture, his chair sponsored by the Granada Foundation, was Arnold Weddle (1924-1997). He was trained as an architect but started a practice specialising in landscape in 1957. He complained that too many architects ignored their sites or expected them to be flat and were reluctant even to visit. *'A good landscape arises out of a sensible appreciation of the restraints and opportunities which the site offers'*, he claimed in 1987, *'Landscapers do a design based on the report, architects write reports to justify the design'*.[100] Besides heading a prize-winning landscape practice now remembered for the Drax power station and Heriot-Watt campus, Weddle was highly active in the Landscape Institute and in landscape publishing.[101] His Sheffield department pioneered new courses embracing ecology and natural science. By 1982 it had six full-time lecturers, the same number as Town and Regional Planning.

The great advantage of grouping these burgeoning departments in a Faculty of Architectural Studies lay in the overlap of subjects concerned with the built environment, encouraging mixed courses and interdisciplinary contact. The prospectus claimed *'Opportunity is offered for graduates to engage in postgraduate research into any branch of know-ledge within the scope of the Faculty.'* It also demonstrated to the outside world the university's unique strength in hosting this group of disciplines, while the creation of dual courses encouraged a new breed of practitioner with a foot in each camp. The first was 'Architecture and Town and Regional Planning' in 1985. It was followed by 'Structural Engineering and Architecture' in 1995, and 'Architecture and Landscape' in 2001.

Following Professor Page's retirement in 1984, the Department of Building Science was reabsorbed into Architecture, but the other three departments continued as the Faculty of Architectural Studies until 2006, the Deanship alternating between them. All were then subsumed into a larger more anonymous body for purely administrative reasons, in an apparent state of amnesia about the advantages of a meaningful academic identity.

Student work of the early 1960s

The architecture-led faculty prospectus of 1965 included three student projects selected by the school as the best of their time which offer a significant sample. They were from the second, third and final year respectively, the subjects being housing, a students' hostel, and a large arts centre. The increasing scale shows the school's continuing intention to engage progressively more complex projects. All are drawn in pen and ink with stencilled lettering, typical of the anonymous perfection sought both in publications and by large architects' offices. Buildings are presented in plan and section without much clue to context, except that the hostel has dramatically changing ground levels. All are essentially object-like and show a concern with expressing the nature of materials, made all the clearer in the case of the arts centre by a photograph of a very textured model. The 'New Brutalism' was much in vogue, Banham's defining book already in production for release the following year.[102]

The housing by Brynley Hughes (opposite top) has a neat completeness about it, dutifully following cramped Parker-Morris sizes with all the furniture drawn to scale, but with rather too generous a frontage prompted by the double-bay plan concept. This solid-void alternation would set up a pleasant rhythm on the street, contrasting with the more enclosed line of courts behind formed by projecting garages. The contrast between brick base and rendered upper floor is much enjoyed, and the unadorned front door is helped out by a vertical slot of window above. Glazing of the living room onto the street in total denial of privacy is a typical error of the time, savagely satirised in Jacques Tati's film *Playtime* which appeared just two years later in 1967.

The student hostel by D. Fingland (opposite), intended to take over sloping Villa land near Sheffield's Botanical Gardens, envisaged six residential blocks set at varied angles to south and west. Like Park Hill they had streets in the air, linking them horizontally to a higher placed social block behind. The service towers on the backs of the blocks recalled the work of Louis Kahn or James Stirling, but the construction envisaged

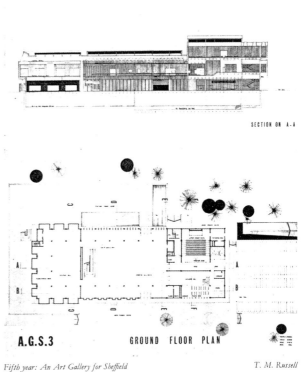

SECTION ON A-A

A.G.S.3   GROUND FLOOR PLAN

Fifth year: An Art Gallery for Sheffield   T. M. Russell

large scale precast concrete elements rather in the manner of Howell, Killick, Partridge, and Amis. The project was evidently chosen because of the student's mastery of three-dimensional thinking in coping with all the changing angles and levels.

The final year arts centre by T.M. Russell (above) was also intended for a Sheffield site, though the reproduced drawings do not identify where. Model and section reveal a concern for various rooflights in the manner of the Finnish architect Alvar Aalto, and the lack of windows suggests it was a standard white-box type of gallery, little related to the outside world. A great ramp in the galleried central hall suggests some drama, but the absence of upper plans leaves us guessing about how it progresses. The student had become deeply engaged with the concrete construction, its textures, projections and cantilevers, and the rhythm of its cladding. The image seems now rather forbidding, but fits in naturally enough to a period that produced works like the Greater London Council's Hayward Gallery or the adjacent National Theatre by Denys Lasdun.

45

81. John Allan's third year 'special study', a dissertation on the British Modern Movement entitled *The Unknown Warriors* 1969.

82. (below) Allan's definitive monograph on Lubetkin, published by RIBA Publications in 1992.

Opposite, first year work from the student portfolio of John Allan.

83. (opposite top) 'Colour Juxtaposition', January 1967.

84. (opposite middle) 'Environmental design, space, tone, and colour', October 1966.

85. (opposite bottom) 'Interior Perspective', October 1966.

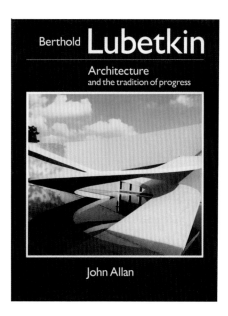

Student experience of the late 1960s

The creation of the Faculty and the break away from dependency on Arts prompted the creation of a new set of courses starting in 1965 which Andrew Beard, a student in 1965-70, called a 'seismic change'.[103] A broad and experimental first year course on Bauhaus lines was devised, followed by new second and third year courses culminating in a BA. A compulsory year out came next, followed by two years to Diploma, the pattern that has remained in place until today. According to Beard, Professor Needham was not much in evidence, the prime mover in the renovation being first year master J. Marshall Jenkins, aided by a recently appointed cohort of young lecturers including John Tarn, Geoffrey Broadbent and John Wilson. There was an emphasis on contemporary arts, and Beard remembers Broadbent bringing in his hi-fi equipment to expose them to John Cage's music. This group of staff also introduced the second/third year 'special study' under which each student chose a topic in one of four sub-disciplines of town-planning, interior design, building science, or history. Beard pursued a town-planning study, so laying a foundation for further studies in that direction and paving his way to the post of Sheffield City Architect, which he held from 1990 to 2000.

John Allan, who arrived as a law graduate from Edinburgh in the following year, 1966, also developed a distinguished career out of his 'special study'. As the first student ever to pursue the history option, he embarked with John Tarn's guidance on a project about the English Modern Movement, resulting in a document 70 mm or so thick which went far beyond the scope of the 18% of the course that it represented. He studied the buildings of leading figures from the 1930s and interviewed them. Maxwell Fry asked to read it and promptly recommended a publication contract, but the task proved too broad. Instead Allan turned his attention to the most sophisticated of British Modernists, Berthold Lubetkin, and took his time – all the while also in daily practice – to explore every nook and cranny of the Lubetkin oeuvre and to discuss it with its author. The result was the definitive 600 page Lubetkin monograph, a work far more technically informed than most art-histories.[104] With this expertise, Allan soon found himself engaged in conservation projects for Lubetkin buildings, and started the restoration wing of Avanti, the distinguished practice of which he is now a director. Allan says he often feels caught between two worlds: *'a theoretician in an environment of muddy boots, but the crass practitioner in a historians' or academic environment,'* but his bridging between the two is surely a virtue. He quotes Lubetkin: *'Practice without theory is blind, but theory without practice is barren,'* and reflects: *'You can't decide what you're going to do until you've learned the history of it – that's how I was taught.'* Looking back, he describes the school in his time as *'very grounded'*:

What was special about Sheffield was that you were set real problems for which real answers were expected ... places like the AA were very clever but did not have a handhold in reality.[105]

John Allan retained all his student work and has generously allowed us to reproduce samples of it. The first impression given by his portfolio is of much drawing for very many purposes, and immediately to quite a high standard. This included accurate sketching of buildings and street scenes, a measured drawing, a fully set-up perspective of a room with furniture, studies in sciagraphy (shadow projection), and numerous technical exercises about precedent, composition, form and colour, all neatly presented on large sheets. The students were being taught to think always with a pencil in hand, and if a drawing could be made to help present some point, it was done. There were surveys of tools, of street furniture and of modern chairs (p 48), each requiring shaded perspective drawings in ink along with a hand-written critique. All this was in addition to the many standard types of drawing normally involved in architectural production: plans, sections, elevations, details, perspectives, mostly carried out in ink on tracing paper with anonymous stencilled lettering.

The technical side was stressed from the start, for Allan was obliged within a month of entering the school to produce a full working drawing of a garage extension (p 50). The final first year project was also fully detailed. Then the main project at the end of second year, a design for 'The Stag Public House' in Sheffield's Psalter Lane, was the subject of a gruelling working drawing schedule of no less than 20 large sheets, including foundations, ducts, and all the wall and roof junctions (p 51). Nowadays this is not even attempted in third year. Construction studies were also pursued in other ways, like an axonometric drawing showing 19 different joinery techniques (p 48), and a surprisingly sophisticated design for bookshelves in folded steel (p 50).

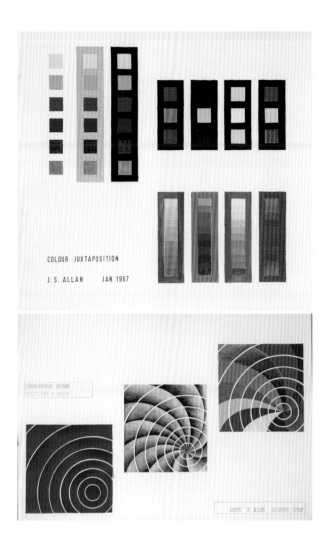

COLOUR JUXTAPOSITION

J. S. ALLAN   JAN 1967

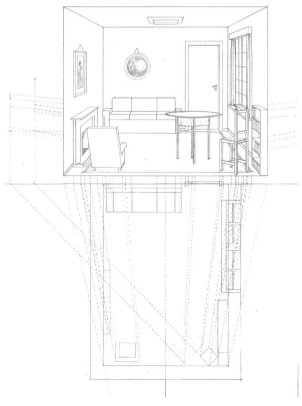

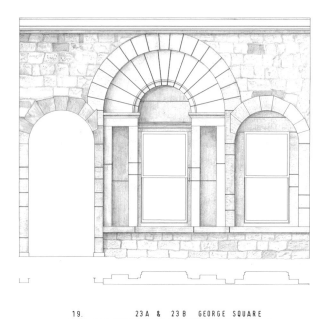

19.   23A & 23 B   GEORGE SQUARE

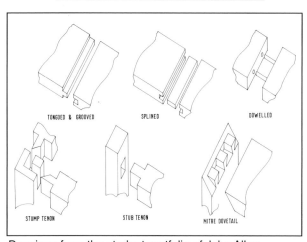

TONGUED & GROOVED   SPLINED   DOWELLED

STUMP TENON   STUB TENON   MITRE DOVETAIL

Drawings from the student portfolio of John Allan.
86. (top) Measured drawing, Edinburgh, summer 1967.
87. (above) 'Joints in woodwork' March 1967, six of 19.
88. (below) One of a series of tools drawn with comment.
89. (top right) 'A study of chairs' March 1967, one of five on the sheet.
90. (mid right) 'Planar study'
91. (bottom right) 'Studies in sciagraphy no. 1' November 1966.

HAMMER. THE OBVIOUS SHAPE FOR
AN IMPLEMENT OF THIS FUNCTION.
NAIL EXTRACTOR VERY EFFECTIVE.
CAST IRON. ECONOMICAL IN DESIGN
AND MANUFACTURE. AESTHETICALLY
COLOURLESS.

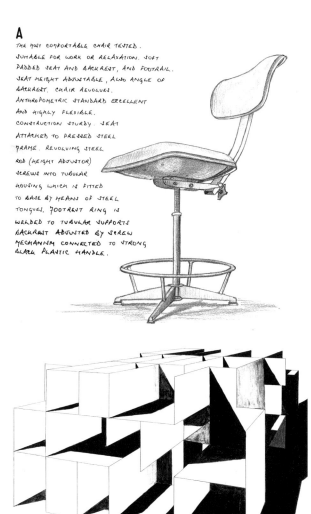

A
THE MOST COMFORTABLE CHAIR TESTED.
SUITABLE FOR WORK OR RELAXATION. SOFT
PADDED SEAT AND BACKREST, AND FOOTRAIL.
SEAT HEIGHT ADJUSTABLE, ALSO ANGLE OF
BACKREST. CHAIR REVOLVES.
ANTHROPOMETRIC STANDARD EXCELLENT
AND HIGHLY FLEXIBLE.
CONSTRUCTION STURDY. SEAT
ATTACHED TO PRESSED STEEL
FRAME. REVOLVING STEEL
ROD (HEIGHT ADJUSTOR)
SCREWS INTO TUBULAR
HOUSING WHICH IS FITTED
TO BASE BY MEANS OF STEEL
TONGUES. FOOTREST RING IS
WELDED TO TUBULAR SUPPORTS
BACKREST ADJUSTED BY SCREW
MECHANISM CONNECTED TO STRONG
BLACK PLASTIC HANDLE.

PLANAR STUDY   JOHN S. ALLAN

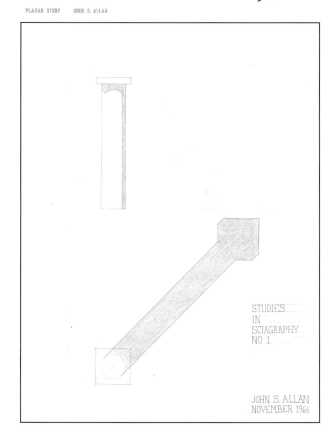

STUDIES
IN
SCIAGRAPHY
NO 1

JOHN S. ALLAN
NOVEMBER 1966

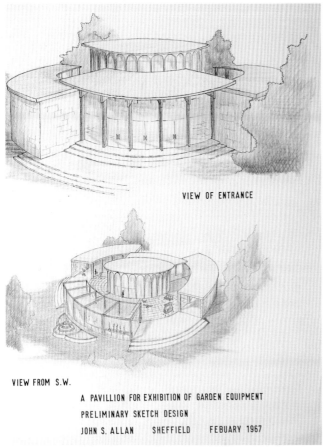

VIEW OF ENTRANCE

VIEW FROM S.W.

A PAVILLION FOR EXHIBITION OF GARDEN EQUIPMENT

PRELIMINARY SKETCH DESIGN

JOHN S. ALLAN   SHEFFIELD   FEBUARY 1967

display 2

display 1

display 3

ADDITION [fusion of elements]

display 1

display 5

display 4

display 2

display 3

JUXTAPOSITION [interpenetration]

92. Sketch design for a pavilion, February 1967.
93. (below) Final design version, March 1967.

94. (above) Two among several plan drawings exploring composition and proportion through the pavilion project.

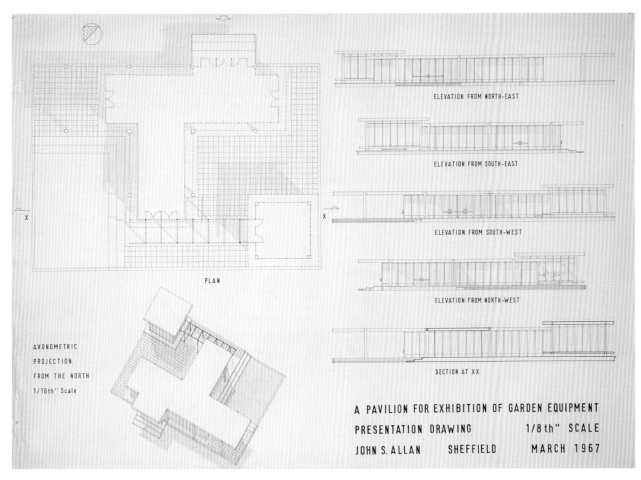

PLAN

AXONOMETRIC
PROJECTION
FROM THE NORTH
1/16th" Scale

ELEVATION FROM NORTH-EAST

ELEVATION FROM SOUTH-EAST

ELEVATION FROM SOUTH-WEST

ELEVATION FROM NORTH-WEST

SECTION AT XX

A PAVILION FOR EXHIBITION OF GARDEN EQUIPMENT

PRESENTATION DRAWING   1/8th" SCALE

JOHN S. ALLAN   SHEFFIELD   MARCH 1967

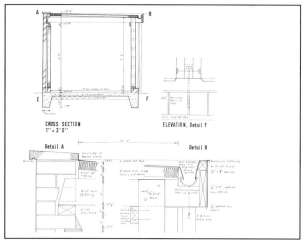

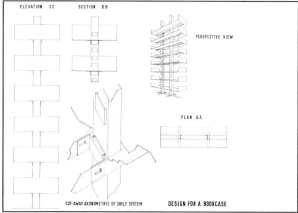

Work from the student portfolio of John Allan.
95. (top) Drawing for a garage, detail, November 1966.
96. (above) 'Design for a bookcase', March 1967.
97. (below) Perspective of a new front for Cutlers' Hall, May 1968, second year.
98, 99. (opposite) General plans and one of the detail drawings of 'The Stag Public House', second year, the subject of a whole working drawing programme.

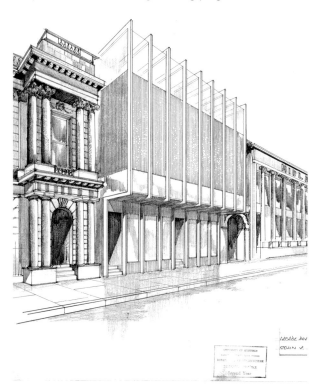

A functionalist ethos is reflected in some ergonomic studies of lecture hall chairs, a graph of anthropometrics, and in the commentaries of some subsidiary studies, such as a beautifully drawn claw hammer (p 48) accompanied by the comment: *'hammer: the obvious shape for an implement of the function. Nail extractor very effective. Cast iron. Economical in design and manufacture. Aesthetically colourless.'*[106]

But at the same time there was a strong implied aesthetic to the teaching based on the virtues of geometrical composition and good proportion. Apart from drawn studies of golden mean rectangles and hyperbolic paraboloids, there were studies of balance and composition throwing up various precedents, and some of these related directly to projects. In February and March of their first year, Allan and his fellow students were asked to design 'A Pavilion for exhibition of gardening equipment' which seems to have been an empty vehicle for compositional study, as no rakes or lawn mowers appear in the drawings, and nor is any site indicated. Inspired by a precedent study which included a 'centralised' building type, Allan at first offered a round building with a daringly eclectic arched central structure (p 49, fig 92), but he seems to have been warned off at a crit and persuaded into a more sober rectangular Miesian solution indebted to the Barcelona Pavilion (fig 93). Attached to this revised project were a pair of compositional studies showing further variants of the plan, one applying various proportion systems – 'golden mean, Fibonacci series, double-cube, progression of squares'; the other called 'Unity' and comparing 'Addition (fusion of elements), Juxtaposition (interpenetration), Dominance (size) and Division (subdivision of a single shape)' (fig 94). The relative virtues of the nine different plan versions are now hard to distinguish, and the compositional exercise seems to have brought no clear solution, though immersion in the issues was doubtless of value.

Allan's final first year project was for 'An artists' colony' overlooking a Scottish loch (p 52). He produced a scattering of little studio houses in stone with crow-stepped gables and a northlight roof. Typical of the brief for a student project of that time were the choice of a remote 'natural' site and the idealistic hermit-like luxury of the artists, whose potential for togetherness seems somehow to have been ignored. Looking across the portfolio, none of Allan's BA projects seem to have had much real social content, though both the pub and the

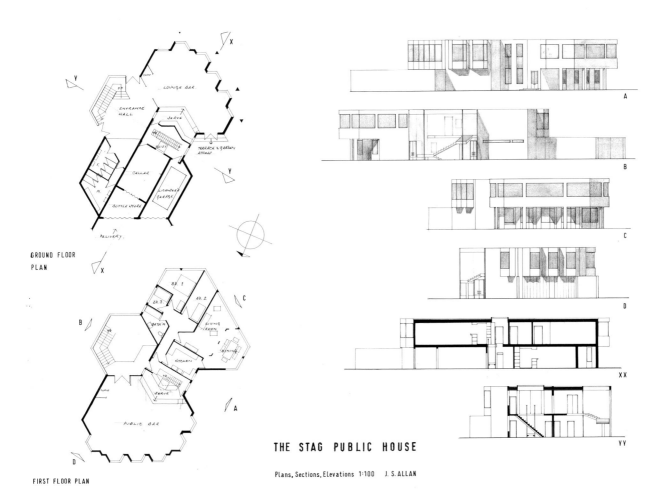

GROUND FLOOR
PLAN

FIRST FLOOR PLAN

THE STAG PUBLIC HOUSE

Plans, Sections, Elevations 1:100   J. S. ALLAN

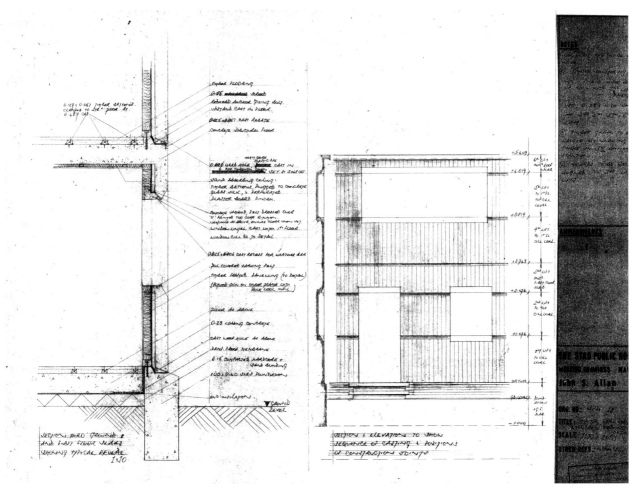

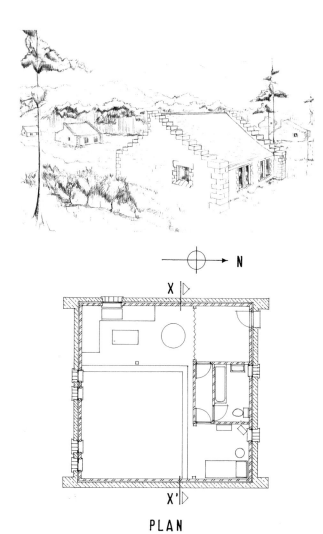

PLAN

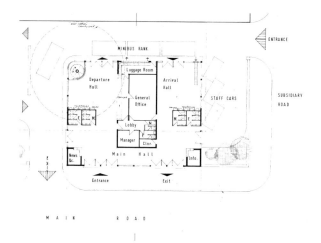

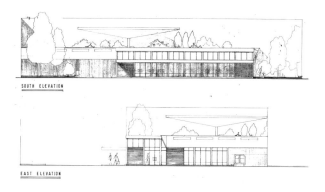

SOUTH ELEVATION

EAST ELEVATION

primary school in second year could have offered it. The third year brought a riskily futuristic heliport (a type that has not materialised), a remote and again utopian holiday island, a comprehensively detailed archaeological museum sited over a Roman Villa, and finally a regeneration scheme for Sheffield canal basin. The failure to engage the social side of architecture more deeply may perhaps be attributed to the narrow definition of 'functions', so much taken for granted in that era, or to the undoubted pressure of completing a design quickly in order to get on with all those working drawings. Allan himself went on to address the social gap in the teaching by producing at diploma level a huge thesis project exploring the unfashionable topic of housing, but his social concerns cannot have been left unmarked also by his historical work with Lubetkin. His practice Avanti has for 25 years been a pioneer of socially sensitive buildings.

A final glimpse of the school from John Allan's perspective is his memory of SUAS, the Sheffield University Architectural Society run by students, which seems to have started in the 1940s and was in full swing by his time. As one of its committee, he personally invited several notable speakers, including Maxwell Fry, Jack Pritchard, Isi Metzstein and Andy Macmillan, Owen Luder, Richard Rogers, David Wild, John Weeks, and Trevor Dannatt. He also invited future head of school David Gosling, then at work on Irvine New Town.[107]

More work from the student portfolio of John Allan.

100. (top left) Final first year project, 'An Artists' Colony', perspective and studio plan.
101. (bottom left) Second year project for a heliport, October 1968, plan and elevations.
102. (below) Second year project for a holiday island.
103. (opposite top) Third year project for an archaeological museum at a Roman Villa, sections.
104. (opposite mid left) Archaeological museum plan.
105. (opposite mid right) Final third year project for redeveloping Sheffield Canal Basin, model.
106. (opposite bottom) Canal basin, plan.

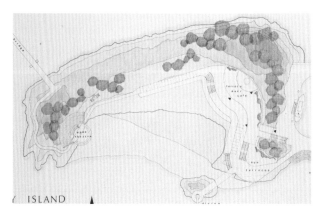

ISLAND

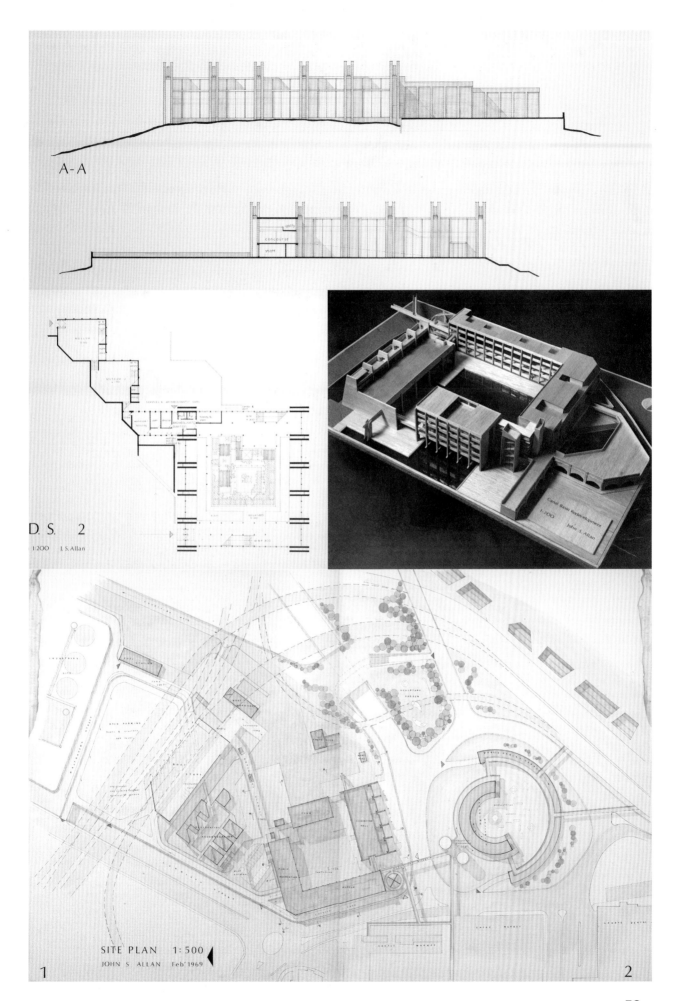

A-A

D. S. 2

1:200   J. S. Allan

Canal Basin Redevelopment
1:200
John S. Allan

SITE PLAN   1:500 ◀

JOHN S ALLAN   Feb' 1969

1

2

107. George Grenfell-Baines (1908-2003), founder of Building Design Partnership, and professor and head of school at Sheffield 1973-79.

108. (below) Grenfell-Baines's competition entry for the Rhodesian Parliament, his final year thesis project at Manchester which gained third prize and launched his practice.

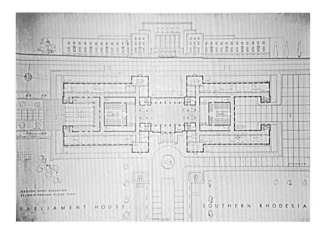

Grenfell-Baines and Integration with Practice

With 173 full-time students in 1966,[108] and an improved staff-student ratio of 1:9.6 (it had been 1: 12.5 in 1950), the school was running well with a growing reputation. The next change of leadership occurred in 1971 with the retirement of John Needham. George Grenfell-Baines (1908-2003), the founder of Building Design Partnership (henceforth BDP) had been approached for advice about the successor. He had nursed an ambition to improve the relationship between teaching and practice, producing a paper on the subject in 1966, and his flattering comparison with the way this was done in medicine went down well with Vice-Chancellor Hugh Robson and his deputy, both of whom had started their careers in that subject. To push these ideas through, he offered to take the job on himself, and though at 63 he had almost reached retirement age, he was enjoying the height of his reputation (dubbed Sir George in 1978), and was perhaps too good a catch to refuse. A three year contract was negotiated. The appointment was controversial among the school's staff, but Grenfell-Baines outflanked them by making their approval a condition of his acceptance.[109]

The son of a Preston railwayman, Grenfell-Baines had entered architecture as an office clerk before starting studies at Manchester University at the age of 28. His thesis project, an entry for the Rhodesian Parliament competition (below left), won third prize, and he used the money to set up his own practice in Preston which immediately took off. By 1947 it had five branches in the north, and he was the only northern architect invited to contribute to the Festival of Britain, designing the Power and Production Pavilion (opposite). By 1959 he also had an office in London, but the Preston one still topped the letterhead. In 1961 the whole enterprise was renamed BDP. Through the 1960s and 1970s competitions were won and one large project followed another – hospitals, company headquarters, university buildings – so that by 2003, BDP had the largest turnover of any architectural firm in Britain.

The change of name from Grenfell-Baines and Hargreaves to Building Design Partnership, dropping the presence of principals, reflects the ethos of the firm and of all Grenfell-Baines's activities. A committed socialist, he sympathised with Gropius's ideal of team-work,[110] recognising both the need for inter-disciplinary collaboration and for equality between architects, engineers, landscape architects, interior designers, cost consultants and others – all brought in-house to offer a seamless and efficient service. He pioneered profit-sharing, paid holidays, pensions, and sabbaticals long before others, and he eschewed the idea of a 'house style', instead encouraging a diversity of approach and giving each designer his or her head. The sense of social responsibility was strong, and an obituary commented that: *'In later life, he lamented the modern architectural education that encourages flashy, superficial gestures without any underpinning technique.'* [111] His remark of 1980 that *'I think of architecture as an airline business – and in that context, aerobatics is irresponsible nonsense,'* might even be considered a bit killjoy.

As the leading figure among northern architects, Grenfell-Baines was a good figurehead for the school in its constant struggle to maintain a high reputation in a strongly London-centred profession, but he was no mere figurehead. Anne Minors, in the school from 1973-79, remembers him as *'a man with a lot of largesse, very generous with the department.'* [112] He pursued his conviction about reconnecting architectural teaching with practice, and took the years-out in training much more seriously, organising them as an acknowledged part of the curriculum, and instituting regular staff visits to the offices in which year-out students were working. He started The Design Teaching Practice connected with the school, and it carried out many jobs such as a health centre in New Mills and some sheltered housing in Chesterfield.[113]

It allowed students to work as they studied over two years,[114] with blocks of teaching time incorporated in the timetable. Work programmes were devised for the students to make sure that they experienced all parts of the process. Barry Maitland, who had been an architect in Irvine New Town and later joined the school staff, was brought in to run it. This office went on independently until 1982, when it was absorbed by BDP as their Sheffield branch. At the same time Maitland moved away to take the headship of the Newcastle School in Australia, and he later enjoyed a second career as a best-selling crime novelist. Never before or since – for the idealistic programme gradually lapsed after Grenfell-Baines retired first from the school and then from practice – was a commercial architects' office so geared to an educational purpose. It is a memorial to Grenfell-Baines's time that we still refer to our final years as fifth and sixth, instead of fourth and fifth as most schools do.

109. Grenfell-Baines's contribution to the Festival of Britain, London 1951, the Power and Production Pavilion.

110. (below) Power and Production Pavilion, stair detail.

55

Three local examples of work by The Design Teaching Practice.

111. The Social and Applied Psychology Building 1988.

112. (below) The Endcliffe Crescent Flats 1992.

113. (bottom) The Stephenson Building 1991.

David Cash, now one of the directors of BDP, joined the school as a student in 1970s, and his experience reflects how the burst of energy witnessed by John Allan five years earlier had already abated, for some of the key figures had moved on to greater things elsewhere.[115] First year teaching by the older staff, including Professor Needham's own lectures, seemed to him dry and remote, textbook stuff: only Alec Daykin really stood out as enthusiastic and memorable. Grenfell-Baines took over as Cash entered his second year, and *'all of a sudden lots of new things happened – it had been run like a teaching institution, out of touch with practice, they had been doing it a long time.'* [116]

The new prof gave lectures in a more conversational style, his wife Milena chipping in as she changed the slides, and students were invited into open discussion. He used his contacts to bring in outsiders – memorably controversial was a student society lecture by Richard Seifert, who in the event chose to talk largely about conservation. The general change of direction coincided with retirement of longstanding staff, leaving room for an influx of new energy. David Gosling was brought in as the second professor in 1973, a practitioner fresh from planning Irvine and Runcorn: Bryan Lawson arrived uniquely qualified as an architect with a doctorate in psychology. Austin Peter Fawcett, Peter Graham Fauset, Alan Craven, Roger Harper, and Cedric Green were all taken on as lecturers under Grenfell-Baines between 1972 and 1974.

Cash remembers an intensive series of building visits, to places as far away as Cambridge and two or three times a term. He also remembers Austin Peter Fawcett coming two or three times to his Bristol office to visit him during the year out, a luxury unimaginable today. Most of all, however, Cash remembers the introduction during his final year, 1975-6, of a series of distinguished visiting critics, which he sees as a result of the Grenfell-Baines revolution, but was essentially the doing of Baines's protégé David Gosling, already by then in charge. When he departed in 1975, Grenfell-Baines instituted the idea of a rotating headship for the school – a deliberately less hierarchical form – which shaped its leadership for the next two decades. It was held in turn by David Gosling, whom he had appointed, and by Kenneth Murta, who had served as sub-dean to the Faculty and was promoted to the chair that Grenfell-Baines vacated.

The Gosling/Murta Period

Kenneth Murta and David Gosling alternately ran the school until 1991, Murta from 1976-77, 1981-85, and 1988-91; Gosling from 1977-81 and 1986-88. Trained at Newcastle, Kenneth Murta had worked in that city and for a short time in Nigeria before he arrived in the school as a lecturer in 1962. He had found some initial success as a practitioner, taking part in a team that gained fourth prize in the Sydney Opera House competition and reaching the final stage of planning competitions for Carlisle and Telford, but the big job never arrived. As a lecturer at Sheffield he helped Professor Needham build St Luke's Church and later built St John's on his own account, developing a special expertise in ecclesiastical work including alterations, maintenance and restoration. He took on the secretaryship of the Ecclesiological Society and editorship of its journal. He also played a role in The Design Teaching Practice, advising on the design of the Social and Applied Psychology Building which opened in 1988 (opposite top). As head he was an effective committee man, engaging himself in university business as Dean, taking the Chair of the Yorkshire RIBA, and later becoming Chair of the ARCUK Board of Architectural Education. That his educational philosophy had been shaped by Grenfell-Baines and remained totally in sympathy with those ideas twelve years later is clear from his article 'Sheffield Studies' published in the RIBA Journal in 1986.[117] The whole discussion, which runs over three pages, concerns the relationship between theory and practice and the integration of practical training within the university course. The illustrations show a student, Caroline Buckingham, at work with Sheffield alumnus Chris Liddle in the firm Hutchinson Locke and Monk, and the results of her detail work in buildings produced by that firm.

David Gosling (1935-2002), had studied at Manchester then at MIT and Yale in the United States. He was deputy chief architect for Runcorn and chief architect for Irvine before taking up his Sheffield chair. He was not unknown to the school, for he had lectured at the invitation of the student society SUAS.[118] One of his most successful students, Stephen Proctor, described him as:

A man of great physical presence and charisma...
yet his artistic talents and ambition came – as is so
often the case – with a personality of complexity
and extreme emotion. There was warmth and
encouragement... but also volatile outbursts, often

114. Kenneth Murta at the time of his appointment as professor, 1974.

115. (below) Competition entry by Kenneth Murta and Associates for Liverpool Cathedral, 1961.

116. (bottom) Church of St John in Park Hill, extension by Kenneth Murta, 1969.

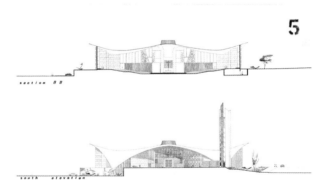

CATHEDRAL OF CHRIST THE KING   LIVERPOOL

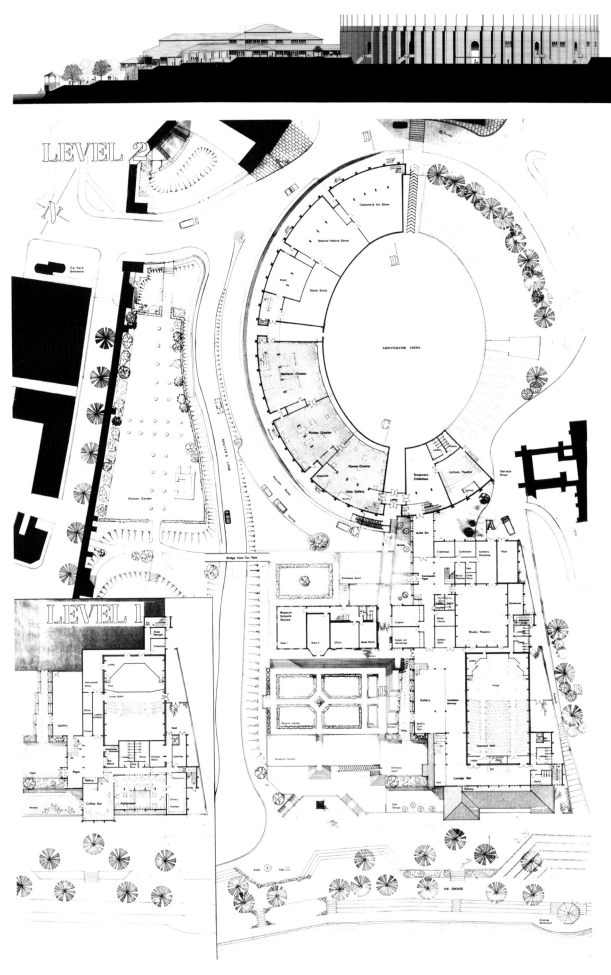

LEVEL 2

Car Park Entrance

Costume & Art Store

Natural History Store

Plant

Stone Store

AMPHITHEATRE ARENA

Roman Garden

SOUTER'S LANE

Access Road

Medieval Cloister

Roman Cloister

Roman Cloister

Undercroft

Aisle Gallery

Temporary Exhibition

Lecture Theatre

Service Road

Buffet Bar

Bridge from Car Park

Terrace

Craftsman Craftsman Scenery Workshop Plant

Common Foyer

Entrance Court

Staff Chair Store

Crèche Music Library

Studio Theatre

Gallery Store

LEVEL 1

Museum Schools Service

Base 1 Base 2 Office Mask Room Public Art Workshop

Gallery Exhibition Balcony

Stage Manager

Conductor

Lobby

Gallery

Instrument Store

Void

Store

Lobby/Exhibition

Lower Stalls

Void

Telephones

Green Room

Store

Gents

BOR's Staff Room

Lobby Stage

Choir Vestry

Play Area

Seating

Kitchen Store

Chef Cloak

Pericon's Garden Pool

Concert Hall

Coffee Bar Restaurant Servery Kitchen

Sculpture Terrace

Gallery

Lounge Bar Balcony

Entrance Court

Café Terrace

Kiosk TCR 1

THE GROVES

Existing Bandstand

58

117-120. Anne Minors, final year thesis project (distinction) 1979 for an arts centre reusing the Roman arena at Chester.

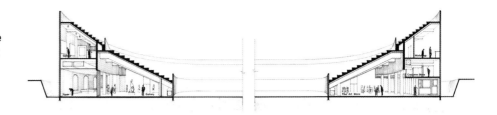

121. David Gosling becomes professor in 1973.

122. (below) Gosling's books. At Gosling's instigation also, Cullen received an honourary doctorate from the university in 1975.
123. (bottom) Gosling's thesis project at Manchester, 1956, already shows his allegiance to 'Townscape'.

124, 125. (opposite) Final year thesis project by Stephen Proctor and Alan Soper, 1985, replanning a large area of London's Docklands, visiting tutor Michael Wilford. One external examiner wanted to fail it for lack of technical detail, but it gained a distinction.

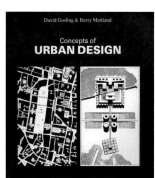
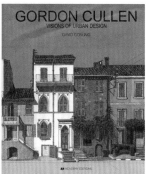

in pursuit of the values he passionately believed in. But this was always tempered with a sense of humour which endeared him to colleagues and students.[119]

Anne Minors described him as *'approachable, affable, available to students... even in first year'* and as *'somebody who was passionate about their interests and certainly pushing the urban design agenda'*.[120] Gosling's interest in urban design had been inspired at first by his friend Gordon Cullen, the theorist of 'Townscape' in *The Architectural Review*,[121] and later by the Rationalist movement of Rossi and the Krier brothers which accompanied the post-modern reaction against isolated object-buildings.[122] This ethos is clearly expressed in the book *Concepts of Urban Design* written with Barry Maitland and published by Academy Editions in 1985. Gosling had met Maitland when both worked at Irvine, and they were staff members at Sheffield together from 1976-82. Under Gosling students were encouraged to consider their projects in a broader context and at larger scale, even to the point where an external examiner protested at the lack of architectural detail, but in compensation three students won urban design prizes.[123]

Gosling's most important innovation was the establishment of a teaching system mainly in the final thesis year,[124] which involved the participation of a very distinguished series of visiting critics, exploiting the personal connections he had developed as a planner. They constitute almost a Who's who of British Architecture during the 1980s, including Kenneth Browne, Gordon Cullen, Louis Hellman, Jack Lynn, Michael Wilford, David Rock, Ivor Smith, Peter Aldington, Terry Farrell, Andy Macmillan, Peter Cook, David Allford, Ted Cullinan, Ron Herron, Patrick Hodgkinson, Chris Liddle, Frank Newby, Michael Neylan, Cedric Price, Vernon Gracie, Brian Anson, Colin Stansfield-Smith, Chris Cross, Wayland Tunley, Eldred Evans, Barry Gasson, Peter Moro, and Ian Ritchie.[125] These luminaries did not just drop in to give the occasional lecture. Many of them came three times a year for four full days at a time, concentrating mainly on the thesis projects of the final year students, and moving around the studio from board to board.[126] They were wined and dined by Gosling and Murta in the evenings when they met and got to know each other, so it became a kind of architectural club, perhaps the reason they were prepared to give so much time year upon year. The visits to the pub have become legendary, but at lunch time students too were involved and the

DOCK  CITY·
URBAN   FRAMEWORK 1

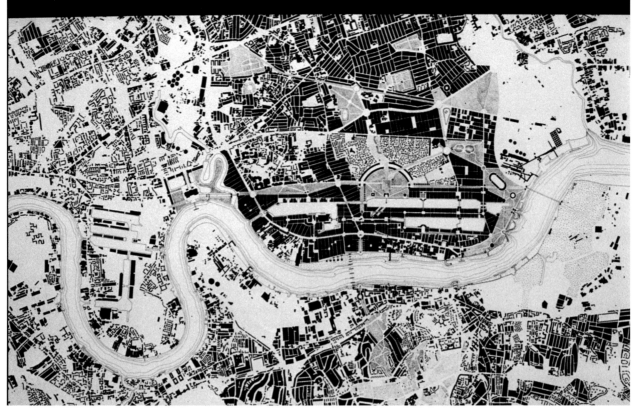

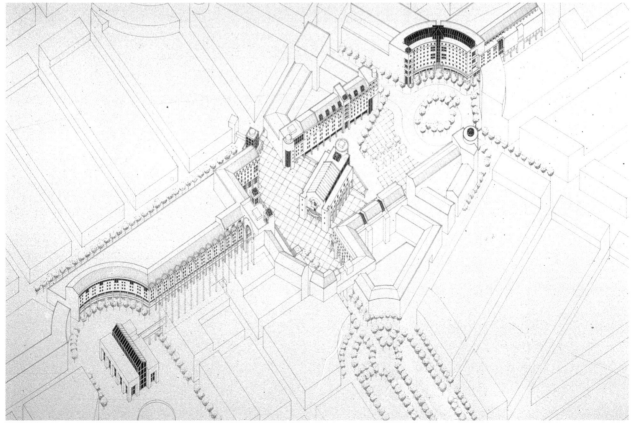

NEW BUILDINGS IN THE
PIAZZA
ROVETTA
BRESCIA, LOMBARDY

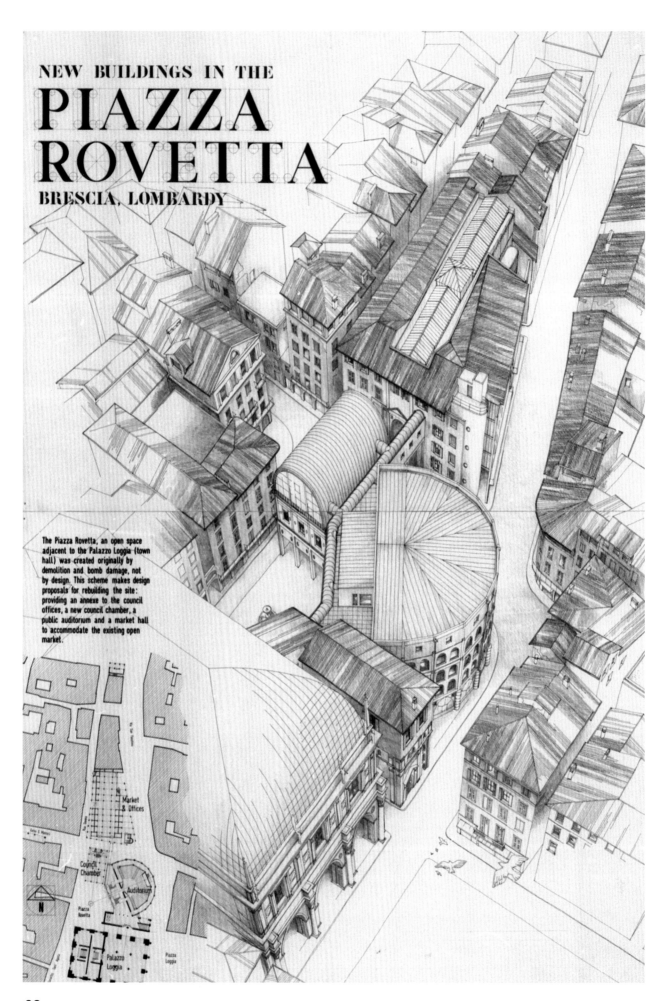

The Piazza Rovetta, an open space adjacent to the Palazzo Loggia (town hall) was created originally by demolition and bomb damage, not by design. This scheme makes design proposals for rebuilding the site: providing an annexe to the council offices, a new council chamber, a public auditorium and a market hall to accommodate the existing open market.

Market & Offices

Council Chamber

Auditorium

N

Piazza Rovetta

Palazzo Loggia

Piazza Loggia

126-129. Greg Penoyre, final year thesis project for an urban intervention in Brescia, Italy, 1981, axonometric projection and elevation drawings. The photograph (right) shows how the drawings and models were displayed at the final presentation.

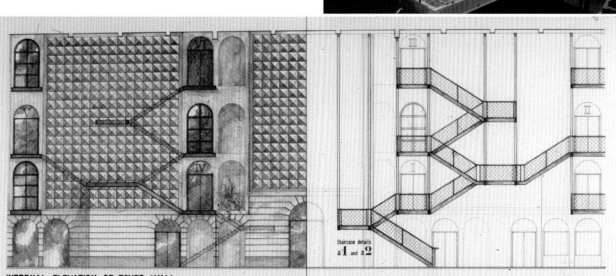

INTERNAL ELEVATION OF FOYER WALL

Showing on the left the mural painted on the plaster wall surface
and on the right the suspended steel staircase
hanging in front.

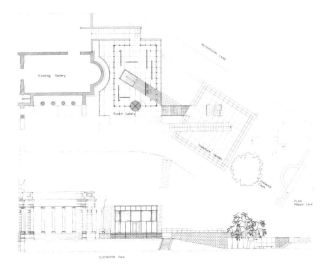

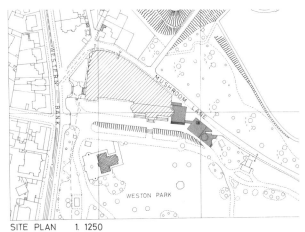

SITE PLAN   1. 1250

130-132. Simon Allford, final third year project of 1983 for extending the Mappin Art Gallery, Western Park, Sheffield. The upward axonometric drawing below reflects the then nationally prevalent influence of James Stirling.

133-137. (opposite) Bill Taylor and Russ Davenport, final year thesis project for Fantasia fun park in London's Docklands 1982. In content and presentation the influence of Cedric Price and Archigram are obvious. The postcard bottom right is signed 'Ron and Nancy'.

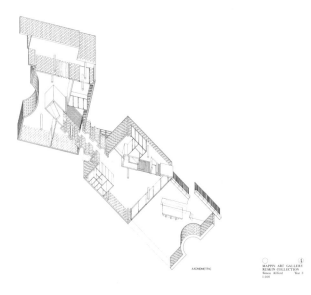

discussion continued. Greg Penoyre remembers an encounter with Cedric Price when he had been unwise enough to mention his enthusiasm for Italian Rationalism. *'What do you mean by rationalism?'* boomed the inimitable Price, who did not find the work of Aldo Rossi in his terms rational at all.[127]

But during the days the critics worked hard, and each was expected to deliver a summary of what he or she had seen on the Friday afternoon.[128] For the thirty or so per year privileged students it gave a boost to the final project, increasing the range of architectural possibilities and putting them in touch with current architectural fashions. As David Cash remembers:

It was wonderful, it was fantastic: the calibre of them! We couldn't believe it – my perception and that of my colleagues was that they enjoyed it too... There was a kind of buzz about it from the dialogue that was developed. It was an uplifting student experience, but also singled Sheffield out.[129]

The school gained not just the prestige of association with these leading figures but also a steady award of student prizes from the RIBA, at that time the main public measure of a school's excellence. The effect was felt right through the school. Simon Allford, now of Allford Hall Monaghan Morris, started in the school in 1980 but moved on to the Bartlett after gaining his BA, so never undertook the thesis project. He remembers an especially strong and friendly studio atmosphere in the Arts Tower, the place glowing like a beacon at night. There was much interaction between the years, with a lot of casual contact and tutorials from staff members who happened to be passing. He did not see much of Gosling because the professor was ministering to the upper years, but a sense of that serious work ahead trickled down through the school as the crucial drawings and models were seen in preparation. On the other hand, in the BA of that time there was what Allford saw as a lack of proper crits: one handed in one's work, it was stamped and marked by the staff behind closed doors, then a few selected examples were shown to illustrate why one piece had been awarded an A and another a C. You had to graduate and become a senior student before being granted the luxury of an open debate on your work.[130] This must only have added to the ritual and mystique of the 'thesis project' as the culmination of the architect's education.

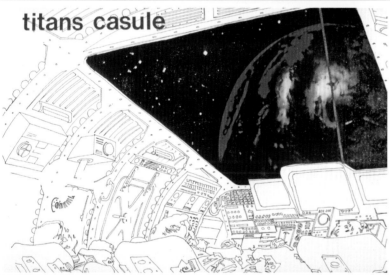

titans casule

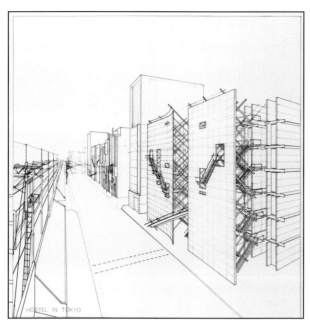

138-140. Sean Affleck, final year thesis project for a hostel in Tokyo 1988, tutored by visiting critic Ian Ritchie.

141. (opposite) Jeremy Dickman Wilkes, final year thesis project for an arts centre in Barbados, 1983, mixing high-tech and vernacular influences.

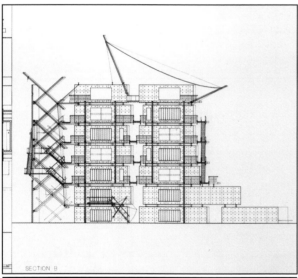

As well as assuring the primacy of the 'thesis project', the visiting critics system could actually become the starting point of a career. Sean Affleck, in the school from 1982-88, was tutored in his final year by Russell Light and by visiting critic Ian Ritchie, winning both the RIBA's Silver Medal and the university's Chancellor's Medal. He went on directly to work for Ritchie, then over many years for Norman Foster, and is now a leading figure in Make, the progressive profit-sharing practice that broke away from Foster under Ken Shuttleworth.[131]

For the periods when visiting critics were not present, the final year students were allotted to staff tutors from across the school, while Peter Graham Fauset and Jim Hall were at different times in charge of fathering the year, sorting out the conflicting advice from different critics, clearing up technical details, and seeing them through. The staff/student ratio was luxurious, but for the thesis project to have worked out so well, the background teaching through the lower years must also have been relatively solid and comprehensive. The studio teaching was full and thorough. Bill Taylor, in the school 1976-82, and now the longest serving architect in the Hopkins practice apart from Michael Hopkins himself, remembers that after the inspiring and broad Bauhaus-based first year, with more art than building design, came an extremely tough second year:

The second year was the year where you were up all night every night working. It was a real sweatshop with relentless projects and the staff were hard, withering with their tongues and without mercy. But not many people left the course – only one or two out of 45. The work ethic came out of that year.[132]

At the end of his third year, Taylor was recommended by 'Gozzo' (Professor Gosling) for a year-out job in the West-Indies, which he now looks back on as: *'the best year anybody could ever want, as a development for me as an architect it was fantastic.'*[133] Later, installed in Hopkins's office as job architect to the Mound Stand at Lords, he was invited back to the school as a visiting critic and recruited several Sheffield students to Hopkins. This example shows the longstanding impact of Gosling's network.[134]

The school maintained a good technical standard. Although without undergraduate students of its own, the Department of Building Science was on hand to provide a solid scientific grounding and technical expertise in materials, climate and physical issues.

AERIAL SITE PERSPECTIVE

MUSIC DEPT.

external
theatre

V I E W   O F   N E W   S Q U A R E

142-145. John Moran, final year thesis project for an urban intervention in Edinburgh, 1986, winner of the RIBA Silver Medal.

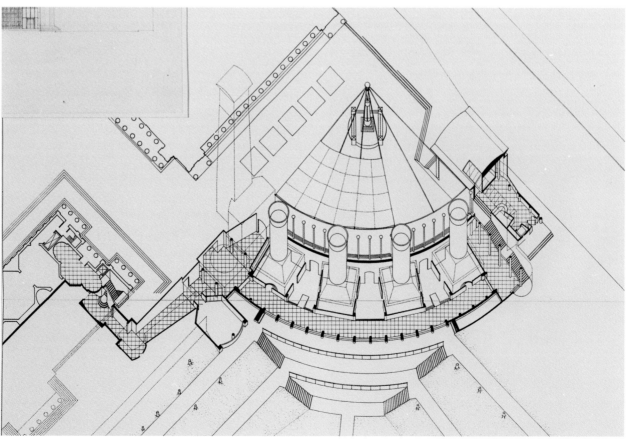

69

146. Cedric Green, SHED solar house project under construction 1974.

147. (below) Cedric Green working at his computer with drawings of his Gleadless housing behind.

148. The young Bryan Lawson working on GABLE with a student.

Following the oil crisis of 1973, technical innovation came also from studio teachers concerned with energy consumption and what we now call sustainability. The pioneer in this direction was Cedric Green who had worked for John Penn in Suffolk.[135] He joined the staff in 1974 and immediately built SHED (solar heated experimental dwelling), a low cost passive solar house which was completed in the next year, its energy performance subject to detailed analysis. Further solar projects followed, culminating in the Sheffield Solar Building Cooperative of 1980, a collaboration with the City Council resulting in 14 solar houses in Gleadless built in 1983-6, one of which was inhabited by Green himself. He reports that *'students were also quite involved in that project, getting hands-on building experience and following it through my tutorials etc.. But the other staff at the school at that period were not supportive at all and I was very disappointed.'*[136] Green had risen to the rank of reader by 1985, but left the university two years later to pursue an alternative career as artist and draughtsman in France. His interest in low-energy housing – which continues until today – was shared and extended by Robert and Brenda Vale, who had worked with Alex Pike in Cambridge on the Autarkic House, and were on the staff in the school between 1984 and 1991.

The 1980s was also a crucial period for the development of computers in architecture, and the energetic Green produced SCRIBE, an integrated system for drawing, graphic three-dimensional display, thermal modelling and passive solar design. It was ahead of its time in using micro-computers rather than large mainframes before the advent of the Personal Computer. An even more ambitious computer project was started by Bryan Lawson in 1978, and became the largest single research and development programme in the history of the school. A forerunner of today's computer-aided design (CAD), it concerned the development of software to support the various ways in which architects produce mental three-dimensional constructs about buildings. It could be read in a variety of ways and extended into simulations of performance, estimations of costs, etc.. With the support of further research grants, it was developed into the university company GABLE, (Graphical Aids for Building Layout and Evaluation) and rights were sold worldwide. Then as computers reduced in size and increased in power, an enormous software market developed and commercial firms inevitably took the lead, but GABLE had paved the way. Lawson was promoted to a chair and made head of research in 1985.

SECTIONAL PERSPECTIVE OF
SUMMER ARRANGEMENT

35

VIEW WEST

149. Cedric Green, design for Paxton Court, Gleadless,
for the Sheffield Solar Building Cooperative, 1983-6.

150. (below) Solar house at Milton Keynes by Robert
and Brenda Vale, 1990.

151, 152. (right) Paxton Court in 2007.

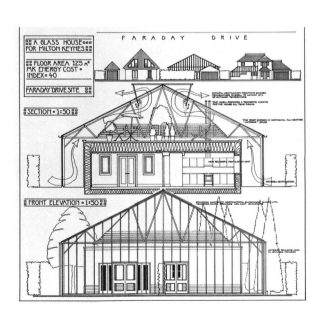

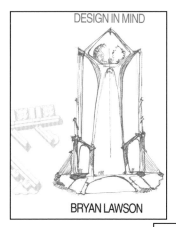

153-155. Books by Bryan Lawson.
Design In Mind 1994;
The Language of Space 1996;
How Designers Think 2001.

156. (bottom) House at Calver by Clive Knights and Russell Light 1991

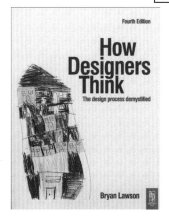

The Lawson Period

In 1990 David Gosling left to take up a job in the United States[137] and the rotating headship fell in 1991 to Professor Lawson. As an architect armed with a Ph. D. in psychology and as an investigator of design processes, he felt the need for a stronger theoretical framework and for more real painstaking research, as opposed to seat-of-the-pants design and the often predominantly visual performance backed by flashy graphics. In the preface to the school's summer exhibition of 1992 he set out his stall, pointing out the rich diversity of the school's output – only some of which took the form of design projects – and encouraging what he regarded as a healthy diversity of style. He also took an ethical stance about research-led teaching:

We defend the fundamental principle upon which university education is based: that students learn best when taught by those who are also actively engaging their minds in the pursuit of knowledge and understanding. [138]

Fortuitously, this change of emphasis coincided with a new national evaluation of universities through the Research Assessment Exercise (RAE) and a consequent increasing pressure to publish and win grants. Success was now found in this arena, with Sheffield the only school in the UK to achieve a Grade Five three times in succession. As it became increasingly clear that the school's resources would depend on RAE performance, it was essential in choosing new staff to find people who had published or would publish, and could offer some specialism beyond the ordinary practice of architecture. On the computer side, Lawson brought in Peter Szalapaj and Chengzhi Peng, and on the engineering side Roger Plank and Olga Popovic, but there were also designers with a more theoretical bent who arrived as Gosling left and Lawson took over. These included three recent graduates from Portsmouth: Russell Light, Clive Knights and Prue Chiles. Light was appointed by Gosling because of his interest in Italian Rational-ism and urban design, while Knights, Gosling's last appointment, had gone on from Portsmouth to an M Phil under Dalibor Vesely at Cambridge, and though he remained at Sheffield a relatively short time, introduced the heavily shaded Cambridge drawing style in opposition to stark line drawings, and brought an injection of Vesely's sceptical phenomenology. Knights and Light designed and built a Neoclassical house in the village of Calver, one of the most distinguished staff buildings of the 1990s (left). The third of the Portsmouth trio, Prue

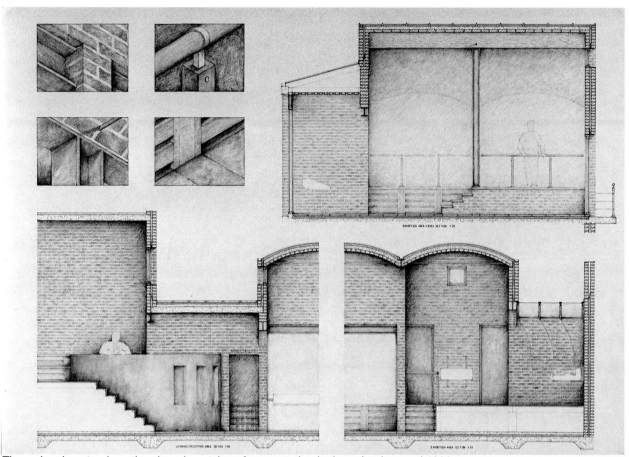

Three drawings to show the changing styles of presentation in the school around 1990.
157. (above) Sections displaying materials and textures by Alasdair Baird, 5th year 1989-90.
158. (below left) Atmospheric drawing on a literary theme by Alex Hall in Clive Knights's first year 1991-2.
159. (below right) Perspective of thesis project 1989-90 by Matt Baker.

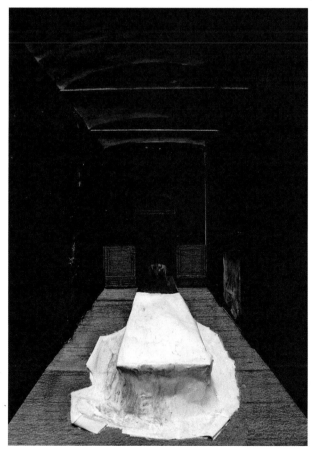

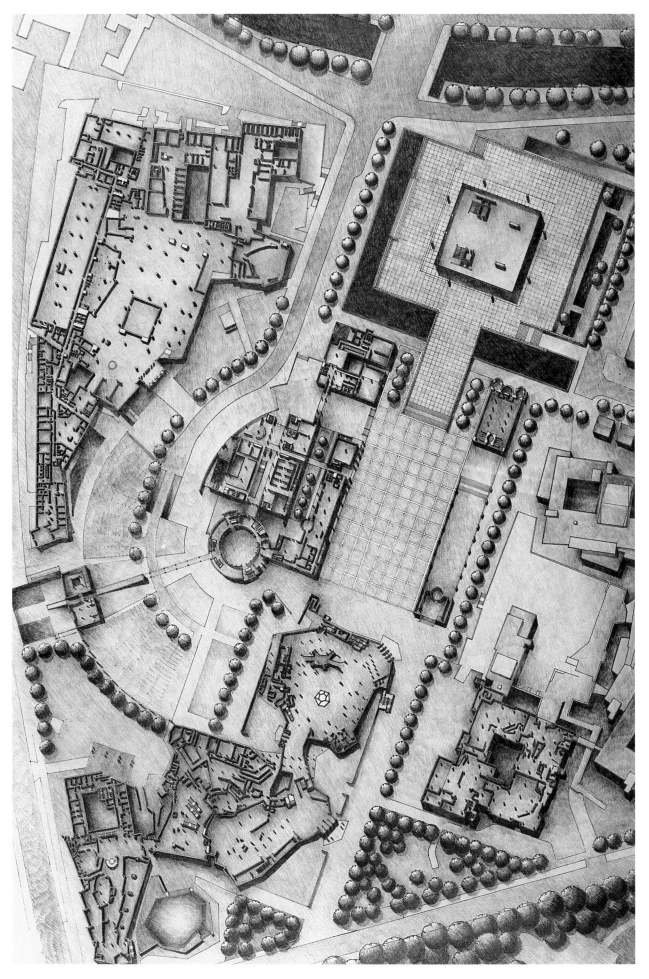

Final Year thesis projects of 1990-91.160. (opposite) Graham Farmer, project for the completion of the Kulturforum in Berlin (Mies's gallery is at the top). 161-162. (this page) Dominic Williams, project for an Arts Centre.

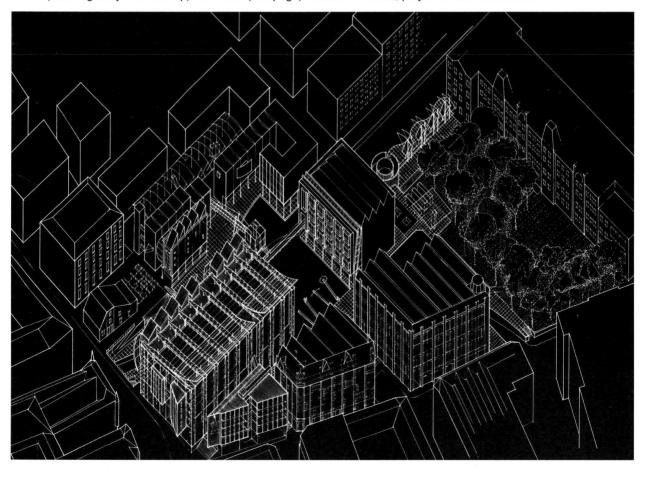

Some staff books

163. Bryan Lawson, *The Architectural Healthcare Environment*, report for NHS Estates 2003

164. Reter Tregenza, *The Design of Lighting*, 1998

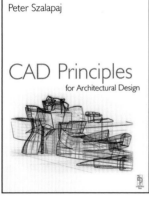

167. Peter Szalapaj, *CAD Principles for Architectural Design*, Architectural Press 2001

166. Olga Popovic Larsen and A.Tyas, *Conceptual Structural Design*, 2003

165. Professor Peter Tregenza.

Chiles, was appointed by Lawson and emerged later as one of the school's most committed and charismatic studio teachers, leading a Diploma studio that repeatedly engaged local social and topical issues.

Under Lawson's leadership, research developed in three interlinked directions: Building Science, Humanities, and Design Processes. The latter he led himself, developing theories of the design process as expounded in his book *How Designers Think*, and through a series of government funded research programmes about building performance involving psychological readings and user measurements. Typical of these studies was a comparison of two hospitals, one in general medicine and one in mental health. They were studied before and after the move into new buildings. Rather than merely canvassing user opinion, measures were taken of apparently independent factors such as patient recovery rates, levels of aggression, and drug consumption, making it possible to prove an objective improvement in performance, and even to put a price on it.[139] This kind of research is performing a valuable service by drawing attention to design aspects that had too often been forgotten in health buildings: the value of view and daylight, quiet and privacy, of buildings that one can navigate without total reliance on signs, etc..

In the area of building science, Professor Page's early retirement left a vacant chair that was filled by the appointment of Peter Tregenza, and a concurrent change of emphasis in the technical side of the school's teaching and research. While Page had been a physicist by training, Tregenza was an architect with mathematical skills and a long research record. He had trained at Newcastle – then part of Durham University – but completed a Masters course at Sydney in 1964, a world leading department for building science, returning to the UK to teach at the University of Nottingham. There he completed a Ph. D. and rose to the rank of reader and acting head. He specialised first in circulation in buildings and later in the provision of daylight, developing new techniques of analysis and prediction, and describing them in books such as *The Design of Lighting*.[140] He also taught regularly in the studio, and contributed to an architectural history course run by Tim Benton at the Open University, never losing the connection between quantitative science and creative design. It was not Tregenza's decision on appointment in 1991 to reintegrate the Department of Building

168. Selma Goker, section through her final year thesis project 1991-2. This beautiful drawing illustrates the intention of that time to show space, construction and habitation at once instead of concentrating on stark line drawings of details. Typical also is the use of shading to show effects of light.

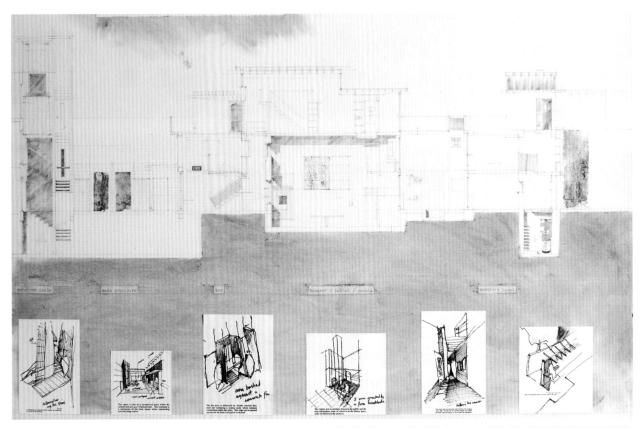

169-171. Satwinder Samra, final year thesis project 1993-4, with impressionistic sketches and collages typical of the period. Samra now runs the school's third year.

Gathered within the space for a meal one looks back to the entrance where leaves of the sycamore tree seem to be whispering inward.

This place enables people to have temporary occupation on the site. By partaking in tea or coffee one brings about a daily ritual.

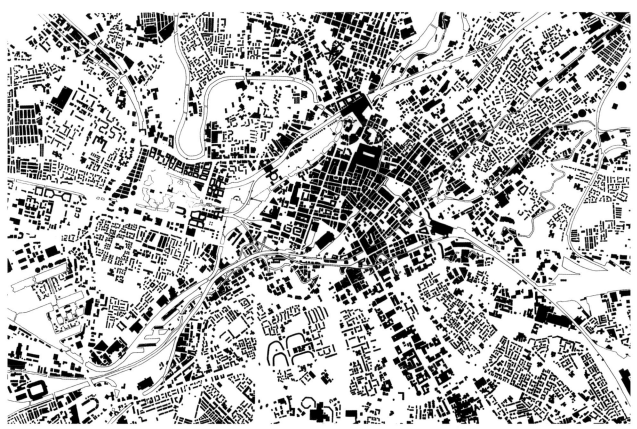

172-174. Dan Jary, final year thesis project for an arts centre in Manchester next to the cathedral, 1991-92. Jary now runs the school's first year.

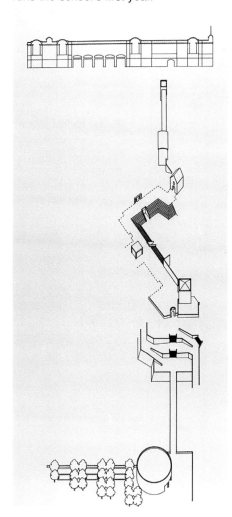

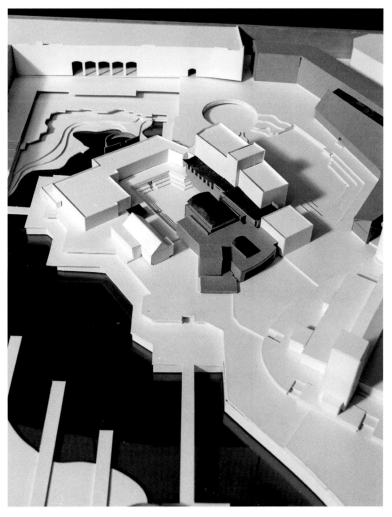

175. First assembly of the Sheffield 1900 model, 1999, from right to left Sheffield Archivist Ruth Harman, Professor Peter Blundell Jones, and Visiting Professor Dan Cruickshank (photo Peter Lathey).

176, 177. (below) Books by Peter Blundell Jones, *Hans Scharoun,* Phaidon, 1995, and *Hugo Häring,* Menges 1999.

178. (opposite top) Model of Hans Scharoun's competition entry for the National Theatre, Mannheim, 1953, built by fifth year students Richard Bradbury, Jonathan Brent, Andy Groarke, Mark Hancock, Chris Milan, Graham Ovenden and Guy Smith for the Hans Scharoun Exhibition at the RIBA, 1995.

179. (opposite middle) One section of the 1:500 scale Sheffield 1900 model showing Lady's Bridge.

180. (opposite bottom) Model of Hugo Häring's Garkau farm, 1925, made by Alan Williams and Rachel Hain for the Hugo Häring Exhibition at the RIBA, 1999.

Science into the School of Architecture, but he was completely in sympathy with Professors Lawson and Murta who had decided to do so, understanding all too well the problems that had arisen in some other schools where the research arm became disconnected from the teaching body, prompting ideological rifts between scientific parts of the course and humanities. It was characteristic of the Sheffield school in the 1990s that these frontiers were regularly crossed and that open debates took place about what was and what was not measurable, and why. The reintegration of building science also reflected the fact that its working conditions had changed, for while in the 1960s the emphasis had been on laboratory experiments involving heavy equipment such as wind-tunnels and artificial skies, the advance of microcomputers in the 1980s and 90s shifted work towards virtual models of ever-increasing sophistication, while web connections brought increasing freedom of location. Continuing research undertaken by the building science team during the 1990s included work on energy by EDAS (Energy Design Advice Scheme) and on the problem of Radon gas pollution.

A bid to stoke up the humanities side of research brought me to the school in 1994, taking up the chair vacated on Kenneth Murta's retirement. I was trained at the AA in London and had built a little, but a teaching career began with an assistant lectureship at Cambridge under Sandy Wilson followed by a period as head of history at South Bank University in London, rising to reader. The Sheffield appointment was probably due my writing: numerous critiques and history pieces in *The Architectural Review* and *Architects' Journal*, and the first book on Hans Scharoun. A publication list was an asset for the RAE, but the texts also provided rigorous material for lecture courses and for post-graduate tuition in accordance with Lawson's concept of research-led teaching. Through the 1990s the stream of books and articles continued, and senior students produced exploratory models for the travelling Arts Council exhibitions on Hans Scharoun and Hugo Häring which I curated with Nasser Golzari.[141] A historical study of Sheffield by the fifth year of 1999 and subsequent years culminated in a large physical model (above and opposite) which provides an unrivalled picture of the city as it stood in 1900 at the peak of its industrial development. This study started a database that is still expanding, an innovative digital version developed by Chengzhi Peng, and it was further extended in three specialised Ph.D.s.[142]

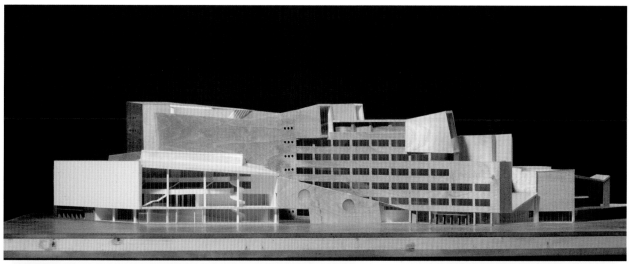

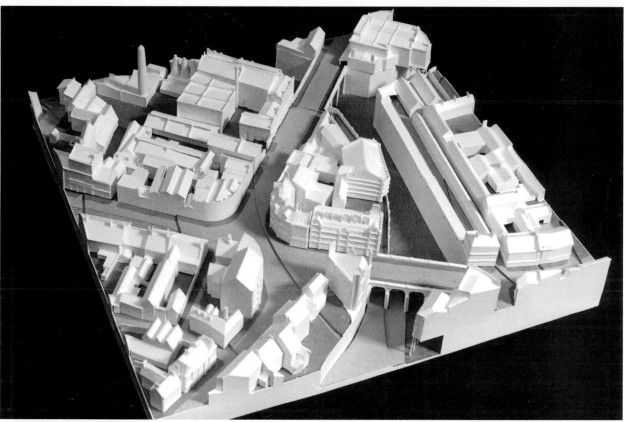

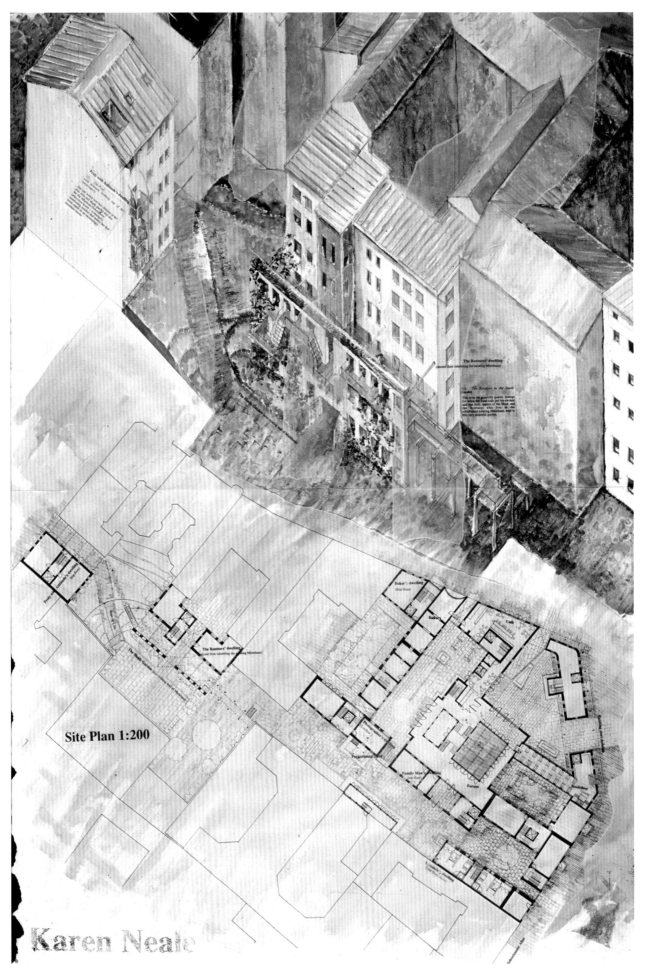

Site Plan 1:200

Karen Neale

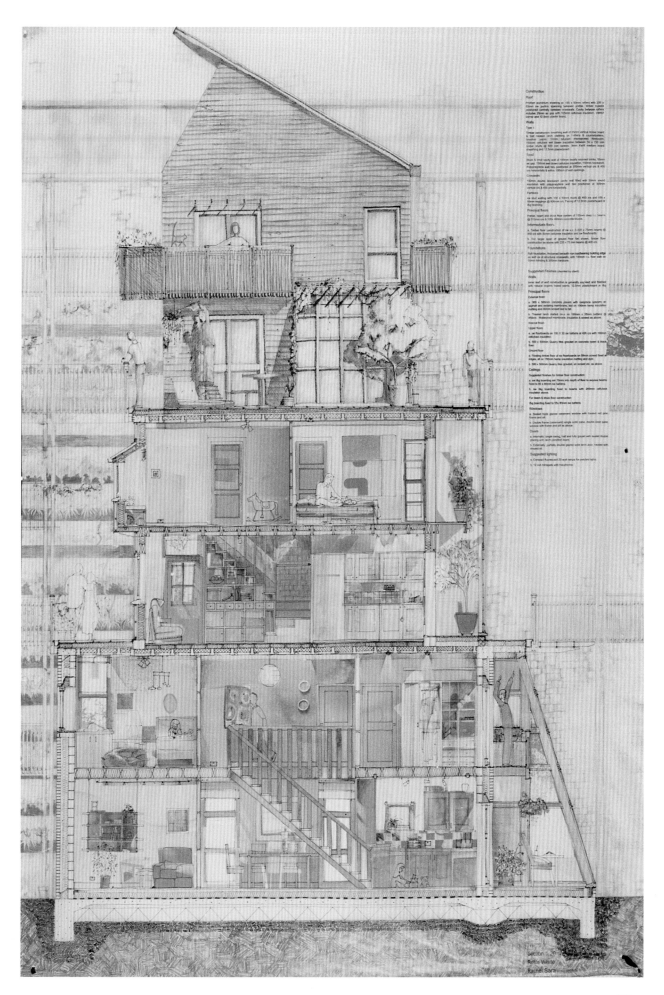

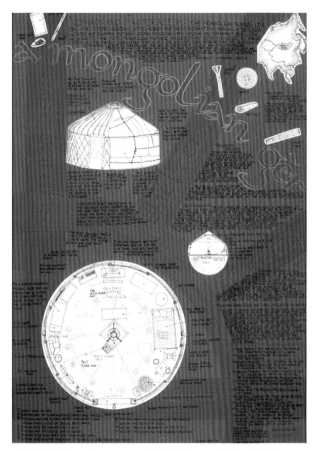

181, 182. (previous pages) Left, Karen Neale, final year thesis project for 'a theatrical Mietshaus' in Berlin 1994-5. Right, Rachel Sara and Rosie White, shared final year thesis project for participative housing in Sheffield, 1997-8. Rosie Parnell (née White) is now a lecturer in the school.

183. (above) First year study sheet examining a Mongolian Ger, in response to lecture course on indigenous architecture by Peter Blundell Jones. Student Martin Lydon, 2004.

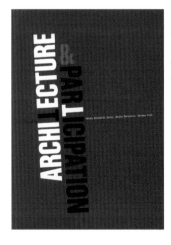

184. Peter Blundell Jones, Doina Petrescu and Jeremy Till, eds, *Architecture and Participation*, Routledge 2005. The book was based on a lecture series with international speakers held in the school in 2002, including Lucien Kroll, Peter Sulzer, Jon Broome and Eilfried Huth.

As the lecturers involved in history teaching retired, we reconstructed what had been a style-based survey course as groups of case studies, and we added an anthropological dimension, looking at what architecture had been before architects got hold of it. For several years we also ran a weekly school forum with celebrity lectures from outside architects and critics, often international. Instead of just giving the habitual lecture about their work, they were invited to address a specific theme each time which changed from year to year, such as 'Architecture and Technology', 'Architecture and Time', 'Architecture and Landscape'. This provoked theoretical discussions which often ended in a lively debate conducted by the students. Among such visitors were Lucien Kroll, Eilfried Huth, Peter Hübner, Shane de Blacham, Volker Giencke, Robert Nijsse, Peter Wilson, Peter Sulzer, Karla Kowalski, Patrick Hodgkinson, Louis Hellman, Peter Davey, Colin St John Wilson, Martin Pawley, Raoul Bunschoten, Florian Beigel, Brett Steele, the film-maker Pat Keiller, the artist Franko B and the anthropologist Stephen Hugh-Jones. The series 'Architecture and Participation' eventually spawned a book with Routledge edited by Jeremy Till, Doina Petrescu and myself.[143] The visiting lecturers were financed by resources that had earlier been devoted to the visiting critics programme, but there were also visiting professors who came for more extended periods to give lectures, tutorials or criticism. They included the engineer Tony Hunt, architects John Worthington and Ken Yeang, and the architectural historian Dan Cruickshank.

Although the increased emphasis on research in the school brought some change of direction, extending the theoretical base and strengthening the lecture courses, much of the work of the school remained studio based, and it became more labour intensive because of increased numbers. In 1990 there were 197 students in the school served by 21 full-time and 4 part-time teaching staff, which produced a staff-student ratio of 1:8.5 without counting technical and administrative staff or visiting professors and critics. In that year there were over a thousand applicants for 35 places, and Kenneth Murta had been arguing for an increase in the quota which was then limited by the university.[144] But Bryan Lawson's preface of 1992 already warned of a threat to resources which could undermine the staff/student ratio, and as the school progressed through the 1990s this became a reality, driven by New Labour's insistence on getting more and more students into higher education. By 1998, just before Lawson handed over to his successor, Professor Jeremy Till, there were 286 full time architecture students in the school and a further 63 in dual courses. Counting dual students as half, and with a full-time staff of 20 and part time of 5, this yields a staff/ student ratio of 1:14.[145] Under Till the numbers went on climbing, so that by 2006 the school had more than doubled in relation to the 1990 figures. Using the same measures, there were 343 full time students and 143 duals to 22 teaching staff and 4 part timers, giving a staff/student ratio 1: 17.3.[146]

The inexorable rise in student numbers put an increasing strain on both teaching and marking just at the time when staff were expected to be increasingly productive of research for the RAE, and to add to these burdens a whole raft of teaching quality measures was gradually imposed over and above the regular RIBA/ARCUK visits. These pressures produced an increasing sense among staff during the 1990s of taking on one hurdle after another, hardly able to draw breath in between, despite relative success and a high reputation in the outside world. One direct effect of increased student numbers was on studio space, which had repeatedly to be rearranged to accommodate them. It became impossible to arrange a permanent drawing place for every student, but the increasing tendency to work on portable computers was already easing the problem, if also eroding the traditional studio culture. Provision of computers for use within the school was another new problem of the period, for the profession was turning over completely to the use of CAD and demanding that assistants have those skills, but the machines were expensive and quickly obsolescent, adding a running cost that had been almost absent a decade earlier. The tendency to conceive work on screen then print it out for presentation introduced a requirement for plotting machines and took an increasing portion of the technicians' time.

Increasing student numbers inevitably meant the use of larger lecture halls and the abandonment of the dedicated ones at the top of the Arts Tower, with concomitant circulation problems. It also brought an increased burden of marking. Yet more difficult to cope with was studio tuition, where 1:1 tutorials had been the traditional pattern. In the undergraduate years various forms of group teaching were invented, with increased student interaction, in the hope that they would learn from each other. In the Diploma School it became increasingly obvious that the year-long self-chosen

185,186. Peter Hübner (above) and Lucien Kroll (below) speaking at the School's Humanities Forum in 2001 and 2002, which gave rise to the Participation book.

final 'thesis project' was no longer effective, for though high-flyers would always succeed, the weaker students struggled to develop convincing research on their own, let alone a reasonable design. The enormous resources that had been devoted to it in the 1980s, involving three separate types of personal 1:1 tuition, were simply no longer available, and there were twice as many students. We decided in 1998 to implement a series of separately led studios each run by a member of staff with a particular agenda, dividing the students between them. This meant not only that the students in a particular group worked on a common theme, but that the staff members involved could explore with them ideas linked to their own research. We tried to assure that they left their separate enclaves from time to time for shared discussions, and the contrast and competition between studios soon became an obvious bonus. The stylistic diversity of the school's design output reflected its open-minded and research-led policy, which was clearly in sympathy with the views of the next professor, Jeremy Till, who took over in 1999.

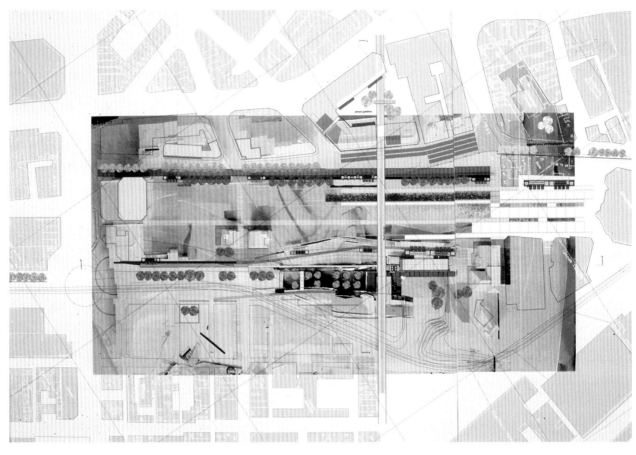

187, 188. Nick Brindley, final year project for a reworking of central Sheffield as an urban park, Prue Chiles's studio 1998-9. The Town Hall is top centre and the Crucible mid right. Layering shows the impact of Koolhaas and Tschumi.

be affecting notions of the home. The drawing shows what was once the physical and social centre of the 'home', the hearth, being replaced by the computer. Are the confines of the home now being removed, the only boundaries now being those imposed by the technology? What makes the home different and how is it defensible in such a context? These conventional home boundaries may become even more challenged if the actual living patterns and uses of the home are altered because of telecommuting and more informal working times. The idea that one is now able to work whilst on the move, whether on the way to work or not, is not a particularly new one. Nevertheless, when adopted as the norm, its ramifications on working life have still yet to be fully explored.

Could it not be that as well as making the office part of a mobile and transient experience, telecommunications also take elements of the home outside their normal realm and put them into to a more amorphous and dissolute context? Further to this, the image challenges whether this preponderance to work/telecommunicate whilst on the move is always desirable or even healthy. Perhaps the 'non-time' of the journey to work is necessary as a stopgap between working and home lives. The thousand yard stare of the commuter may be used as way to pass between the two poles of home and work. In particular, this may be strengthened in urban situations where the worker becomes anaesthetised by a continual bombardment of information.

189, 190. Greg Moss, final year project for a reworking of Sheffield railway station, Prue Chiles's studio 1999-2000: the presentation mixes sophisticated computer modelling with impressionistic collage.

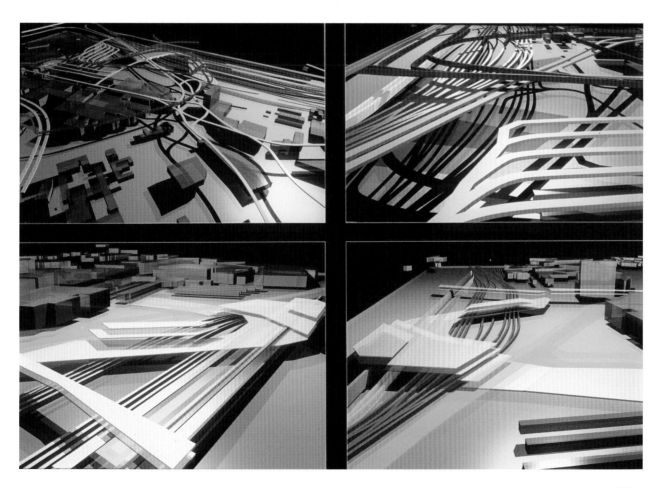

191: Professor Jeremy Till and Professor Sarah Wigglesworth.

Below and opposite, their pioneering straw-bale house at Stock Orchard Street, North London 2001.

192 (below) The concrete-filled gabions and sand-bags on the facade facing the railway.

193. (opposite) The house seen from across its garden which serves as a vegetable patch. Straw bales are visible to left behind the transparent corrugated sheeting, the main first floor living rooms are illuminated behind the glass, and the small library tower rises behind.

The Till Period

Before coming to Sheffield, Professor Till had a made an academic name for himself at the Bartlett school in London. He had also participated in the architectural practice of his partner Sarah Wigglesworth, who simultaneously joined the school as part-time professor. They had just completed their revolutionary straw-bale house in North London, an architectural experiment boldly expressive of social and ecological values. Steeped in the writings of Henri Lefebvre and having completed an MA in Philosophy, Till brought to the school an attitude of intellectual scepticism as well as an increased social and egalitarian emphasis, questioning the architect's elitist role. In his inaugural lecture he criticised the profession's pursuit of glossy and sometimes empty images, and the widespread tendency to concentrate on the golden moment of the perfect photographic image caught between the exit of the contractor and the arrival of the tenant. Architecture cannot afford to be so pure and detached, he argued, it needs to be regrounded in social purpose and considered over the long term, in 'thick time', a duration encompassing both a building's production and its subsequent life. A word often heard from Till was 'contingent', meaning that architecture must necessarily respond to particular conditions of time and place. Space is a social product, he argued, so the interaction of groups and ideologies should be examined, and the conservative view still implicit in much of the architectural world needed to be questioned. Till also stressed the need to look after the planet, since buildings consume about half the world's primary resources in construction, and through their energy usage produce about half the total carbon dioxide emission.[147]

Till's emphasis on social and ecological values and on process rather than product further drove the school towards plurality and experimentation, and towards a deeper understanding of the implications of architecture, rather than seeing the whole effort of architectural education as culminating in the production of pretty drawings for the RIBA's shows. This ethos in many ways continued that of Bryan Lawson, and was typically expressed in the research project Clients and Users in Design Education (CUDE), which had been instigated by Lawson and was continued under Till. The bringing of users into the school to provide a real basis for design projects had happened sporadically for years and had been welcomed by Lawson, but Till gave it a new urgency, encouraging the

194, 195. Live project in Romania, 2005-6, initiated by students and involved with building a school. A subsidiary theme was to humanise the use of concrete.

introduction of regular Live Projects in the Diploma School, building on the earlier work of Prue Chiles. Set at the start of every year, the projects typically involved the construction of playground structures or minor conversions in local schools, as well as more strategic work. Once these got going they snowballed and increasing numbers of clients contacted the school, keen to improve their local conditions and to solve their wider problems through architectural vision and research. For these clients it not only created a facility they might otherwise have missed, but opened up a participative process and gave them a sense of empowerment in their local environment. For the students the primary experience was social, a real interaction with users, but there were also sometimes encounters with tools and materials, with the real world of construction, a down-to-earth kind of practice after years of theory, and not of a kind found in the average office. The projects also encourage group work and the kind of communication skills that are too often missed in the individualistic emphasis of most architectural education. The popularity of these projects with students comes across repeatedly, and some arriving from other schools claimed that they applied to Sheffield precisely because of the live projects. As one of them put it:

What the live projects are good at is making you question your relationship with the client and the way things are done, instead of coming straight into a practice and just going down the traditional route... I think it certainly produces a stronger dialogue that has more of a continual evolving process. The majority of time the clients don't know what they want: they think they want something, but if you take a step back and look at why they want it, there is something completely different, and when you start engaging them with that, it opens up other ideas in their mind and they fly off at another tangent. It encourages you to explore more with them, rather than just answering their call. [148]

Another student claimed:

For the majority of us involved, the Live Projects allowed us the most direct opportunity we had had to deal with clients, let alone determine the nature of this contact. This combination of student leadership and direct client contact allowed a revelation in our understanding of the true value of our work and the ability it has to help the people who need it. I can't praise the

Live Projects enough and it's great to see the expectations of what can be achieved rise each year, as experience and knowledge is passed from those that have participated the previous year to incoming students. Having shown the results of my live projects in job interviews, I can also say that employers are very interested in looking at them.[149]

Re-empowering the user

Less obvious in the outward product of the school were a whole series of revisions to teaching practices that took place under Till's leadership. First gender: there were women students even in the 1920s, but the proportion was very small. It has gradually increased, but only for the first time in 2006/7 have women exceeded men in the first year. In the matter of staff the change has been more dramatic. There were always women secretaries, often underpaid and underrated but with noticeable power even back in the 1950s. The head's secretary – the current longstanding incumbent being the efficient and highly-respected Judith Jackson MBE – has always been the lynchpin of the school organisation. But as far as academic staff are concerned, women were completely absent apart from the occasional part-timer up to the beginning of the 1980s. The male dominance was certainly felt: June Whitham, a woman student of 1942-7 and one of two in a year of ten, reported that Professor Welsh was dismissive of women students' work. In reaction, she persuaded her male colleagues to hang everything at a crit anonymously so that he could not easily pick it out. By the 1970s things had improved, and women students of that period do not report having felt oppressed. Anne Minors felt they had worked harder than some of the men who seemed happy with a mere pass, but the worst instance of gender politics she could recall was the accusation by male students that women gained advantage by wearing skirts at a crit.[150] The staff gender balance began to change in the 1980s, but by 1990 there were still only three women on the permanent staff: Brenda Vale, Melanie Richardson and Mary Roslin. Lawson and Till both strove to improve it by appointing more women as staff and as external examiners, so that by the year 2002/3 eight out of 18 lecturers were women – almost half. Also symptomatic of the period was the appointment of Sarah Wigglesworth as Sheffield's first woman professor of architecture: only the second in the UK.[151] In recent years women have stood out at Sheffield among the most popular and charismatic studio teachers. Judy Torrington, known for her research into social buildings like

196. Live project 2006: composting lavatory in Ecclesall Woods, tutors Prue Chiles and Scott Fletcher. It was runner-up in the RIBA small projects prize.

197. Live project 2006, work with a school in Sheffield.

198-201. Cover and sample pages from *Building Clouds Drifting Walls* by Ruth Morrow, 2003, a booklet describing her innovations in Sheffield's first year.

schools and old people's homes, was long a key figure in the development of First Year and has risen to reader. Prue Chiles, already mentioned, founded the Bureau of Design Research in 2004, a new kind of active office within the school which combines consultancy, research and teaching, as well as pioneering new consultative techniques for architects. Doina Petrescu, a world-leading authority in the field of feminism and architecture, has taken groups of students to Romania and North Africa, working on self-build initiatives with women's groups and local cooperatives. Another crucial female figure at the turn of the millennium was Ruth Morrow, who took on the leadership of First Year and radically restructured the course to challenge both the spoon-feeding expectations of students fresh from school and the demands of an increasingly commercialised profession:

Many of those responsible for recruiting newly qualified architects are dissatisfied with the teaching that students receive. The expectation seems to be that, to be useful to the profession, graduates need only be proficient computer draughtsmen, able to produce working drawing packages for tried and tested building solutions. They should also, of course, be happy to work long hours for little financial reward and hopefully not ask too many questions.
Now place this expectation in the context of the state that the profession is in: a large number of building projects proceed without the input of an architect, and where an architect is involved their role is often marginalised. The architect is not seen as adding value, and is instead viewed as an extravagance. Most architects have had to progressively reduce their fees to a point where the service they can offer is substandard – a vicious circle. If architecture schools produce drawing office fodder in line with these outlined expectations, how can this situation ever change?[153]

Morrow's first decision was to keep alive 'the memory of being an ordinary user' by concentrating on the house and home as the main territory of investigation and design. Her second was to involve clients and outsiders from the outset, bringing them into the studio to set and evaluate projects, and to work when possible out in the city, with real places and real people. The third was to devise projects involving cooperation and group working: typically the design of a valise in cardboard by one student which then had to be built to his/her drawings by another. Each then had the experience of receiving and deciphering drawn instructions as well as handing them out, and the ensuing dialogues about misunderstandings between 'designers' and 'builders' made a conventional 'crit' superfluous. But crits in general had also come under scrutiny, with the institution of a system in which one group of students would judge the work of another group while the staff stood by and observed. This prevented the automatic dominance of tutors' tastes and values, and involved some questioning of the criteria of judgement, even if ultimately the staff had to allot marks. Questioning of the crit had also been part of the research programme CUDE which spawned the book *The Crit* written by Rosie Parnell and Rachel Sara, students in the school who had progressed through doctorates to becoming teachers, taking part in Morrow's studio.[154] Several of Morrow's projects involved real confrontations with materials and techniques, not the proxy ones of copied details applied to putative designs which are the bane of every school. The whole course aimed at a *'creative engagement of reality'* with the assumption that architecture is a social process, always involving other people both in its production and its consumption. The aesthetic in all this is a personal discovery gradually made and *'we should be suspicious of contrived beauty in the first year studio'*.[155] After winning a university award for teaching excellence, Morrow left the school in 2003 to take up a chair at Ulster University, but her innovative courses have been carried on by Rosie Parnell, Stephen Walker, Dan Jary, and others.

The emphasis on research engendered by the RAE (Research Assessment Exercise) had meant a steady increase in the number of doctoral studies undertaken in the school, with more staff eligible to tutor them, but a bold innovation under Professors Till and Wigglesworth was the instigation of a Ph. D. by design. This is a particularly tough prospect because good designers are not generally good theorists and vice versa, but candidates are obliged both to produce design work of high quality and to be able to justify it in detail. This means that value judgements can no longer be left as intuitive but must be properly argued, and that means have to be found to communicate architectural values without reducing everything to reductive quantitative formulae. It requires, in short, that architecture should establish its own nature as a discipline independent from the various arts and sciences to which it contributes, and from which it borrows.

202-203. Cartoons by Mark Parsons illustrating the intimidating nature of the traditional architectural school student review. From the book *The Crit* by Rosie Parnell and Rachel Sara.

Final year project by Leo Care, 2001-2, based in Brezoi,
Romania, and carried out as part of Doina Petrescu's
studio. Care now works for BDR and teaches first year.
204. Section through proposed social centre.
205. (left) Consultation with the townspeople.
206. (below) Drawing about the handling of open spaces
and proposed cultivation.

cultivation consultation

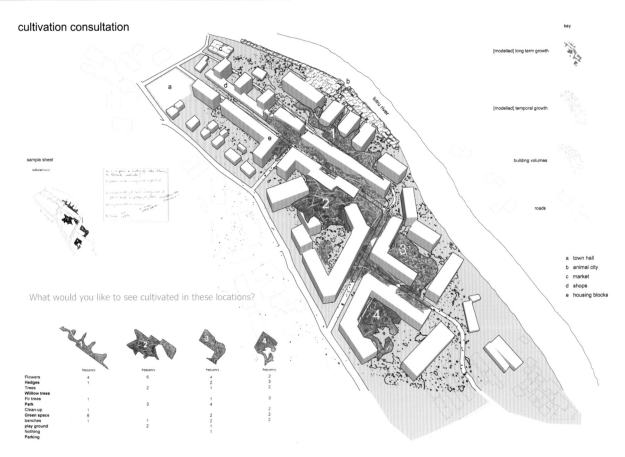

key

[modelled] long term growth

[modelled] temporal growth

building volumes

roads

a town hall
b animal city
c market
d shops
e housing blocks

sample sheet

What would you like to see cultivated in these locations?

	frequency	frequency	frequency	frequency
Flowers	4	6	4	2
Hedges	1		2	3
Trees		2	1	2
Willow trees				
Fir trees	1		1	3
Park		3	4	
Clean-up	1			2
Green space	6		2	2
benches	1	1	2	2
play ground		2	1	
Nothing				
Parking				

207-209. Final year project by Michael Hood, Sarah Wigglesworth's studio 2001-2, for 'Dalston Dining Room' after a considerable study of and engagement with the London suburb.

This work reflects the growing social concern in the school at the break of the new millennium as well as exemplifying a type of presentation that seeks to communicate possibilities and intentions impressionistically rather than representing a hard and fast built product.

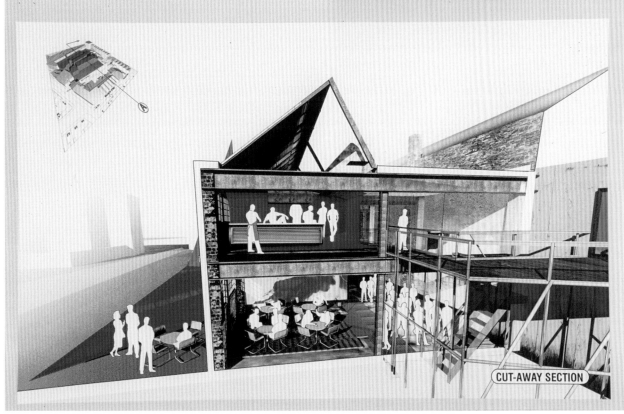

In 2006 Professor Till was invited to organise the British exhibit at the Venice Biennale, where the general theme was 'cities'. He decided to avoid both the usual glossy show of recent architecture and the automatic choice of London as subject. Taking Sheffield instead, he launched an energetic collaboration of artists and designers to represent the city warts and all, at every scale, and with interactive elements. The pompous neoclassical formality of the old pavilion was denied by entering around the back, and the rooms were given themes related to the various scales at which Sheffield could be represented. Installations included situationist walks around the city, oral statements by locals, and invitations to visitors to add to a message board and make collages. The show provoked some scorn and envy from London architects, but certainly succeeded in putting Sheffield on the map.

210, 211. Two exhibits at the British Pavilion, Venice Biennale, 2006, curated by Jeremy Till. Above 1:1 room by the Sheffield arts collective Encounters, below 1:100 room with installation of Park Hill housing project by Studio Egret West and Hawkins\Brown.

The Plank Period
Since 2005 there has been a return to the concept of rotating headship and the school has been led by Professor Roger Plank. Trained as a structural engineer, Plank joined the university's engineering department in 1975, where among other jobs he found himself teaching second year architects. He found that he *particularly enjoyed interacting with them in their design project work where they often posed some tough challenges*,[156] so when offered the opportunity in 1987 to move over to architecture to take charge of the teaching of structures, he took it.

As the bridge between the two departments he helped to set up of the architecture-engineering dual course in collaboration with longstanding staff member Roger Harper. He also developed universal teaching material in a programme instigated by British Steel, and when they offered to fund a new chair of architecture and engineering in 1995 he was the leading candidate and thus a natural choice. On the research side Plank had long been engaged in the development of computer programmes for structural engineering design which were cutting-edge for their time and proved lucrative for the university, but in the 1980s he had also developed a second major speciality concerned with the prediction of buildings' structural behaviour during fire. This has grown to sustain a large research group on the border between architecture and engineering with five full-time staff and 12 research students, which has won many grants and awards. Plank is a world expert in this field.

Plank's headship has coincided with the return to the school in 2005 of Professor Steve Sharples, who had started in the school as a Ph. D. research student in building science under John Page in 1975 and rose to reader by 1998, but was then lured away to a chair at Sheffield Hallam University in 1999 where he became head of its new School of Architecture, Environment, and Technology in 2002. He returned to the Sheffield University school in 2005 to take the building science chair, only its third holder in 40 years. A physicist by training, he has engaged in research ranging across the environmental aspects of architecture, from daylight and thermal performance to ventilation and noise control, involving collaborations with colleagues within the school, in adjacent departments, and at other universities.

Another chair in the building science area is occupied by the acoustician Jian Kang, who was taken on by the school as a promising and much published lecturer in 1999, promoted to reader in 2001, and thence to a personal chair in 2003. He is an international specialist in room acoustics and urban environmental noise control, with several large research projects in progress. The presence among the professoriate of such figures indicates a healthy and perhaps overdue revival of building science, but without internal rivalry or friction, for all work together. Professor Plank makes this quite clear, stating modestly that he *'would not presume to give architectural leadership'* and that he *'took on the role of Head of School in 2004 on the understanding that senior colleagues would provide the detailed pedagogical direction and interface with the profession'*.[157] He maintains the clear and progressive ethical direction established by Lawson and Till, subscribing to the principles of inclusion and pluralism and taking pride in *'the move towards less confrontational reviews of student work, and the engagement of all relevant spheres of society in the design process - something which Sheffield has pioneered very successfully in recent years'*.[158] Roger Plank's policy statement from the beginning of 2007 set goals that all at the school could share:

My ambitions for the School are to see us consolidate our position as one of the top schools nationally and internationally, in both teaching and research. Key factors in this are restoring our working environment to the standards we enjoyed when we first moved into the Arts Tower, providing a wider range of learning experiences and routes to qualification for students, broadening our student intake, and exposing students to the best architectural thinkers worldwide.[159]

212. Professor Roger Plank, current Head of School.

213. (below) Professor Steve Sharples making light measurements with a student.

214 (bottom) Professor Jian Kang setting up an acoustic test (all photos by Peter Lathey).

Conclusion

A School of Architecture is a constantly changing organism as members of staff arrive and leave, bringing and developing their special enthusiasms then removing them to be replaced by something else. The strengths and weaknesses of a school therefore tend to change from decade to decade, if not from year to year. Interviewing alumni from many periods, it was striking how many thought they had participated in a period of exciting change and renewal in a place that had previously been moribund, but this seems mainly to reflect the enthusiasm of new waves of staff and to demonstrate the limits of communal memory. Some periods were more lively than others, but it is hard to identify a dull uncreative period after the Second World War, and the school's earlier struggles were due more to problems of money and recruitment than failure of imagination. Evolution has been constant, but there have also been major shifts of emphasis. Looking back across the century, both the school's role and its size have changed. Started by the local society and the leading local practices, it remained small before the Second World War and, unlike the grander Liverpool, was geared mainly to producing local practitioners. In the immediate post-war period it expanded rapidly along with the rest of the university, educating students not only from across the country but also from overseas, as far away as Africa and Malaysia. By the early 1960s its intended and declared role was national and even international, underlined by the alliance with Womersley, the Sheffield RIBA conference, and the creation of the quadripartite faculty with its expanded expertise.

The importance of connection to London and beyond was by that time well established, and has remained a key factor for the school. Though it had been nurtured by local firms, it grew far beyond them, and the debate could no longer be purely local. An increasing stream of visitors arrived at the station, while the school's own staff could often be seen going the other way. This interchange, most spectacularly exhibited in Gosling's visiting critics programme of the 1980s, has before and since been endlessly fulfilled by visiting professors, lecturers and tutors, and has been the school's life-blood. Exchange of students with other schools has provided further cross-fertilisation.

But if connections with the outside were vital, it has mattered also that the school is in Sheffield. Alumni speak fondly of the city and the legendary

215. First year students being photographed with their cardboard chair designs, year 2003-4.

216. (below) Students mounting the end of year exhibition, summer 2004.

217. (opposite) Mounting the 2004 show: there are still plan and section drawings in the conventional way for some projects, but the shows have become much more like an art installation, using many media at different scales, and also showing evidence of research. It has become much more difficult to encapsulate them between printed pages.

(photos by Peter Lathey)

98

friendliness of its people, while the socialist background of the 'People's Republic of South Yorkshire' is so ingrained as to be hard to avoid. Although the original industrial landscape is now fast disappearing, the evidence of skilled manual work in somewhat primitive conditions used to be visible on every other corner. It has been a gritty unpretentious city, for its size rather short of grand monuments, and with a complex informal street-plan made all the less coherent by ruthless road planning. Its peculiar beauty is only revealed as one becomes able perceptually to peel back the layers and see how it became. Being educated in and making projects for this place must have had a very different effect from attending a noble classical city like Edinburgh, and it helps perhaps to account for the Sheffield school's relative disinterest in style games and purely aesthetic refinement. It is also spared from the London schools' compulsive and competitive fashion parade. The culture-shock of a recent ex-Bartlett student faced with a group live-project was palpable:

When I came to Sheffield I was so used to everything looking beautiful and you designing for things to look nice, and all of a sudden the whole group of seven were saying 'that's not important, that's really not what it's about at all'. And I had to keep telling myself that's not important and this isn't what its about, this is a completely different way of looking at things. [160]

So what is it about? Alumni stress the range and thoroughness of the Sheffield courses and the hard work they were expected to put in. The school has often enjoyed a reputation for technical thoroughness, and it is perhaps telling that several Sheffield alumni have become senior partners in national firms, the kind of key figures who hold everything together. Examples are Bill Taylor at Hopkins, Colin Moses at Robert Matthew Johnson Marshall, Keith Brewis at Grimshaw's, Chris Liddle at HLM Architects, Peter Barbalov at Farrell's, Neil Taylor and Russ Davenport at FaulknerBrowns, David Cash, Martin Sutcliffe and Chris Harding at BDP, and Tony Skipper as head of Mc Aslan's

Manchester office. If for decades Sheffield hardly seems to have produced named founder partners in top national firms, it can now claim among others both Stephen Proctor and Andrew Matthews of Proctor Matthews, Greg Penoyre of Penoyre Prasad, Peter Barber of Peter Barber Architects, Roger Hawkins of Hawkins Brown, and both Simon Allford and Paul Monaghan of Allford Hall Monaghan Morris. Allford's father David, also a Sheffield alumnus from humble local origins, was the leading second generation partner in the national firm Yorke, Rosenberg, and Mardall. On the public side the school produced a Sheffield City Architect in Andrew Beard and a deputy chief architect at Birmingham, Will Howland. Bryan Jefferson, partner in Jefferson, Sheard, and Partners, became President of the RIBA besides producing local work of significance and taking an advisory role within the university. John Fidler became chief architect at English Heritage before moving on to private consultancy, and of course John Allan, already much mentioned, is a national expert in conservation as well as a director of Avanti.

The Sheffield school has also contributed much to architectural education, supplying probably more heads for other schools of architecture than any other in the country. It started when the school's first lecturer, William Purchon, moved on in 1920 to take the headship at Cardiff, but many followed after the war. Jim Howrie left in 1952 to become head at Leicester and later at Birmingham, Marshall Jenkins became head at Leeds, John Tarn at Nottingham then Liverpool, Geoffrey Broadbent at Portsmouth, Austin Fawcett at Queen's Belfast then at Nottingham, Barry Maitland at Newcastle in Australia, Peter Smith at Sheffield Hallam, Peter Fauset at Northumbria, Ruth Morrow at the University of Ulster, Steve Sharples at Sheffield Hallam. Brenda Vale became professor at Auckland in New Zealand. All were former members of staff, but in addition Andrew Ballantyne, current professor at Newcastle, was Sheffield trained, as was Jane Rendell, professor at the Bartlett. Rory Spence (1949-2004) the critic, teacher, and Australian guest editor to *The Architectural Review*, was also a Sheffield student.

Changes in practice

Looking at the whole unfolding story over a century, it is clear that drastic changes in the nature of practice have occurred, many of which are reflected in the nature of the drawings produced. The gentleman-architect of pre-war days was expected to exhibit great skills in pen and watercolour, to set up convincing perspectives, and to have imbibed for instant reproduction a ready vocabulary of styles, but he – and it nearly always was he – could rely on the good honest builder to set the necessary lintels in place and to choose the right size of screws for the door hinges. Traditional construction could be carried through largely by rule of thumb without much calculation, building regulations were almost non-existent, and planning was relatively simple. Ordinary houses and humble everyday buildings could still be carried out by mere builders in a comfortable vernacular, so 'architecture' always supposed something of a flourish.

By the end of the1950s all that had changed, the applied historic styles having been vanquished in favour of what now with hindsight seem somewhat naïve modernist versions, and the teaching concentrated less on precedent than on principle. Impressive for that period is the sheer comprehensiveness of the course, the large number of exercises and studies in form and technique, the ambition towards technical mastery. Life-drawing and measured drawing persisted, but detailed drawings for instruction of builders were expected within first year, while full sets of working drawings were produced by third. It was probably always an illusion to think that a BA student could independently design and execute even a small building, but the ritual of working drawings and large scale details at least exposed them to the whole process. The weakness of the system lay perhaps in the limited time given to the design concept through too easy and pragmatic a 'solution'. By the early 1970s 'Crisis in Architecture' was being declared nationally and internationally,[161] modernist shortcuts were being regretted, and new attention was being given to architecture's rhetorical role.

At Sheffield the early 1970s brought a new emphasis on the need for a link with practice and practical training, but Grenfell-Baines's sincere effort to relink school and office did not last, even if the role of the year-out continued to be taken more seriously. In the post-modernist phase of the 1980s under the joint leadership of Gosling and Murta, the school re-engaged the questions of style and the importance of urban context, bringing student work into the public arena. Never had the school won more prizes or seemed closer to the pulse of national architectural life, but the intense concentration on elevating the production

218. Students from Diploma School Unit 5 mounting their end of year show, summer 2004.

of a few stars was labour-intensive and the results sometimes over-reliant on graphics. The rising student numbers of the 1990s forced staff-time to be spread more thinly, but at the same time relentless demand for visible research sharpened up intellectual debate. The rate of staff publication soared. Enquiry shifted away from how one should construct the putative building, whose presence as the central object of study had hitherto been taken for granted, moving instead to questions of whether one should build in the first place, of whom one was building for and why, of what architecture is as an activity and a political act. All buildings must nowadays be planned by specialists, yet architects have been losing ground to surveyors, facilities managers, construction managers and others in the construction field. All too often architects are marginalised on the basis of their supposed 'aesthetic' contribution, or patronised for their imposition of a certain 'look', a 'designer brand'. But aesthetics in building is not an add-on extra, and the architect's true role is about much more than offering style. He or she is the one professional in the building process who is charged with overseeing the whole cultural process, balancing the value of the place and its memories against the demands of the client, the comfort of the user, the impact on the public, and costs both economic and planetary. It requires some power of imagination, a skill to envisage things, and the growth of a sense of public responsibility. Over five years at a school of architecture there are very many skills to acquire in many specialist fields, but the student must also find his/her own creativity, then learn to subordinate it to the task in hand. Knowledge and training are essential, but much more important is awareness of a wide range of issues and an ability to make sound and intelligent judgements about them.

Notes

1. In 1897 the Sheffield Medical School (1828), the Technical School (1883), and Firth College became incorporated as the Sheffield University College by Royal Charter. The Royal Charter creating the University of Sheffield was granted in 1905. For more detail see Helen Mathers *Steel City Scholars*, James and James, London 2005 (henceforth referred to as Mathers 2005).

2. A couple of short articles in *The Builder* reveal the presence of an earlier but short-lived school set up by the Sheffield Master Builders' Association in 1848 with W.R. Harrison as professor: see Roger Harper, *Some Notes on the Origins of the Sheffield University Department of Architecture*, unpublished typescript dated May 1981 (henceforth referred to as Harper 1981). On the state of UK architectural schools generally in 1910, there is a detailed series of articles *Architectural education at home and abroad* by Alfred W.S. Cross, vice-president of the RIBA, in *The Builder* beginning July 2nd 1910, pp. 3-4. Sheffield is specifically dealt with in Part V, July 30th, pp. 119-120.

3. John Soane charged £50 p.a. in 1784, rising to nearly £200 when he became famous: *Architects' Journal*, 9 October 1974, p. 874.

4. See W.R. Lethaby, *Philip Webb and his work*, Oxford University Press, 1935.

5. For biographical information see Stephen Welsh and J.W. Davidson, *History of Hadfield Cawkwell Davidson 1834-1976*, private publication, (copy in University of Sheffield Library).

6. £5,500 based on the retail price index, £7,100 based on the GDP deflator, but £28,000 based on average earnings: see Measuring Worth.com

7. Indenture document dated 16th November 1910, now in the hands of his daughter, Mrs Sheila Adams.

8. Catalogue of the exhibition *150 Years of Architectural Drawings Hadfield Cawkwell Davidson*, held at Mappin Art Gallery in 1984, p. 82.

9. J. Mansell Jenkinson from the *Reports of the Sheffield Society of Architects* no. 73, 1960-61, pp.11-12. Quoted in Roger H. Harper *The first hundred years of the Sheffield Society of Architects 1887-1987* published by The Sheffield Society of Architects 1987, pp. 10-11, (henceforth referred to as Harper 1987).

10. Also called successively William Flockton, Flockton Lee & Flockton, Flockton & Son, Flockton & Abbott, Flockton Gibbs & Burrows, Gibbs & Flockton, and Gibbs, Flockton & Teather, see Ruth Harman and John Minnis, *Sheffield, Pevsner Architectural Guides*, Yale University Press, New Haven and London 2004, p. 24 (henceforth referred to as Harman and Minnis 2004).

11. Ibid, also Harper 1987, p. 1.

12. Listed by title in Harper 1987, p. 10. They were eventually given to the School of Architecture and some are still in the University Library. The Sheffield School of Art was started in 1843 as part of the national School of Design. Its main building at 55 Arundel Street of 1855 was designed by Manning and Mew. It expanded to take over much of the block. Damaged by wartime bombs, it was finally demolished in 1960. The institution was absorbed into what is now Sheffield Hallam University.

13. Short biography in *The Sheffield University Magazine*, June 1938, vol. 1, no. 2, pp. 85-89. Obituary in the *RIBA Journal* 4th Jan 1936, p. 260, and letters 18th January, p. 313. Apart from the University's Firth Court and Mappin Building, Gibbs designed the Mappin Art Gallery, Ranmoor Church and many other substantial buildings in the city.

14. Harper 1987, pp. 2-9.

15. He visited Harvard, Columbia, MIT, and Montreal: Harper 1981.

16. University archives SUA 5/1/35/9.

17. The drawings were approved in March 1903, while the school of architecture was still merely a proposal. *'On March 2nd, 1903, Messrs. Gibbs & Flockton's plans for the new University College buildings in Western Bank were accepted, the cost being £67,500 exclusive of the Library, which would add a further £7,500 to the total. The area was to cover 11,821 square yards, 8,000 having been purchased for £7,000, and the rest bought for £3,500 by Dr. H. C. Sorby, and presented by him to the College. The buildings planned by Messrs. Gibbs & Flockton were to surround a quadrangle 154 feet by 110 feet, with room for extension.'* From 6-Univ on University of Sheffield website.

18. Harper 1987, pp. 14-15.

19. Information from the RIBA courtesy of Irena Murray and from an obituary in *The Builder* of 18th December 1942.

20. Letter from Charles Hadfield and James Wigfull concerning Edward Gibbs in RIBA Journal, 18th January 1936, p. 313.

21. The Sheffield City Archives hold the Society's records including numerous letters to Wigfull and a collection of early photographs of historic houses in the area.

22. Full name and dates from the Dictionary of Scottish Architects (www.codexgeo.co.uk/dsa/architect) which also reveals that he was in 1898-99 assistant to William Warlow Gwyther (1829-1903) who had practised in London since 1855.

23. See University Calendar 1908-9 pp. 488-499. The curriculum was also reported in an article on the Sheffield school in *The Builder* July 30th 1910, pp. 119-120.

24. University Calendar 1908-9, pp. 488-499.

25. Aston Webb was the architect of London's Admiralty Arch and of the main façade of the Victoria and Albert Museum; Halsey Ricardo was an Arts and Crafts figure best known for a somewhat Byzantine artist's house at 8 Addison Road, Kensington, London, of 1905-7, which has become a favourite setting for period films.

26. *The Architect*, 22nd July 1910.

27. University of Sheffield Library Special Collections MS 281.

28. W.S. Purchon in *RIBA Journal*, 5th December 1914, p. 66.

29. Ibid. I have cut occasional words to shorten it.

30. Innocent and Brown were the main architects for the largest group of Board Schools outside London (see Harman and Minnis 2004).

31. C.F. Innocent, *The Development of English Building Construction*, Cambridge University Press Technical Series, Cambridge 1916. It was reprinted in the 1990s. The copy in the University Library belonged to J. Mansell Jenkinson. Another book including local vernacular examples, and also some recent farm buildings by Hadfield, Gibbs & Flockton, and others, is Thomas Winder, *Handbook of Farm Buildings, Ponds, &c., and their Appurtenances,* Pawson and Brailsford, Sheffield 1908. Winder had been a president of the Sheffield Society of Architects and Surveyors.

32. Henry Beckett Swift Gibbs, born 1889, who joined the family firm in 1921.

33. See Andrew Saint, *Towards a Social Architecture: The Role of School Building in Post-war England*, Yale University Press, New Haven & London 1987, pp. 62-3.

34. A.W. Chapman, *The story of a modern university: a history of the University of Sheffield*, Oxford University Press 1955, p. 314. (henceforth referred to as Chapman 1955)

35. William Rothenstein was a friend of the historian H.A.L. Fisher, Vice-Chancellor of the University from 1913-1917, see Mathers 2005, p. 82.

36. Harman and Minnis 2004, p. 192.

37. Harper 1987, p. 16.

38. Ibid, p. 24.

39. Then The Department of Architecture and Civic Design as part of the Technical College. Purchon's obituary in *The Builder*, 18th December 1942, reports that he *'at once proceeded to build [The Welsh School] up to the healthy and flourishing place it now occupies among the RIBA "Recognised" schools, with an impressive record of successes in awards.'*

40. Verbal information from Professor Richard Weston at Cardiff, remembered from an article by Chris Powell about the history of the Welsh School.

41. *RIBA Journal* 18th January 1936, p. 313: *'As first lecturer in charge of the school of architecture, I spent much time with him in the early days of that school, for which he worked so hard before its establishment in 1907, and which he has assisted in all possible ways ever since. I count it a great privilege to have worked with him in that way, for he was a man of great sincerity of purpose, and one who was exceptionally thorough in all that he undertook.'*

42. University Calendar 1925-6, p.146.

43. He won the competition for the Sheffield War Memorial in 1924, and it was completed in 1925: Harper 1987.

44. Charles Denny Carus-Wilson born 1886, educated at the AA in 1904-5, set up in practice in Edinburgh with Mears between 1928 and 1934 and taught at the Edinburgh College of Art.

45. Harper 1987, p. 25.

46. Harper 1987, pp. 24-25.

47. Ibid, p. 25.

48. Welsh designed and built the University Student Union 1935-6, and won a competition for Lower Shiregreen Church in 1932, for which there were 21 entries. He also designed the conversion of St Mary, Bramall Lane in 1950 (Harman and Minnis 2004).

49. The most detailed source is an obituary by Roderick Urquhart in *Yorkshire Architects* April 1987.

50. See Liverpool School of Architecture Centenary Review, *Architects' Journal* 11th May 1995, p. 60.

51. In his doctoral thesis, *Architectural Education in Britain 1880-1914*, Cambridge 1982, Alan Powers quotes from the RIBA Board of Education Minutes of 1910-13, concentrating particularly on a meeting of 16th February 1911 at which Lethaby and Reilly put forward their opposed views.

52. Harper 1987, p. 18, cited from the reports of the society 1908-9, p. 40.

53. Charles Reilly, *Some architectural problems of today*, Hodder and Stoughton, London, 1924. The copy in the University of Sheffield Library is that of Stephen Welsh, given to him by Reilly as a Christmas present in 1927.

54. Ibid, p. 61.

55. Ibid, p. 61.

56. See *The development of Architectural Education in the UK, Architects Journal* 9th October 1974, p. 874.

57. Prospectus, Department of Architecture, University of Sheffield 1928/9, pp. 4-5 (University Archives).

58. Ibid, pp. 6-7.

59. Sir Banister Fletcher (1866-1953) *A history of architecture on the comparative method for students, craftsmen and amateurs*: first published in 1896, it has gone through more than twenty editions and revisions with various publishers. It remains a standard textbook and definer of the traditional architectural canon despite its many limitations.

60. Harper 1987, p. 25.

61. Ibid, p. 26.

62. For relative student numbers see the graph in Chapman 1955, p. 360.

63. Mathers 2005, pp. 167-169.

64. They are mainly on stretched Watman in ink with watercolour wash – he also made working drawings on linen, but they were long ago discarded.

65. Author's recorded interview with Daykin, Retford, 27th June 2006, and subsequent telephone conversations.

66. From examination records of those years held in the school.

67. Examination records; 32, 36, 35, 31 and 40 students for years one to five respectively.

68. It was converted for new use by Professor Welsh over the summer: Building Committee Minutes 1954.

69. David Allford remembered an occasion when he was being taught by Alec Daykin and Welsh appeared on the gallery overhearing something and shouted: *'Daykin, what on earth are you telling them now!'*. Welsh could be fierce, critical, and impatient, but he could also inspire loyalty and be generous, personally subsidising students who ran into financial difficulty. Alec Daykin, asked why he went back to teach said simply *'he wasn't the kind of man you could refuse'* but remained in the school until retirement. Philip Toft, a student in the early 1950s, referred to Welsh throughout our conversation as 'Stephen' and saw him as a fatherly figure (author's recorded interview with Toft, Wingerworth, 25th July 2006). Toft was not the only one to mention the financial help to students.

70. RIBA Journal Yorks. Vol. 1, No. 8 September/October 1969 *St. Luke's Church, Sheffield*. Includes photographs of the building and commentary on the design.

71. Harper 1987, p. 30.

72. Geoffrey Broadbent 1963-8, later head at Portsmouth; Jim Howrie 1969-74 later head at Leicester and Birmingham; and John Tarn 1963-70, later head at Nottingham then Liverpool. Marshall Jenkins, also on the staff at this time, later became head at Leeds, but he had been appointed by Stephen Welsh.

73. Author's recorded interview with John Allan, London, 31st October 2006.

74. From 1964 the University Calendar ceases to list drawing staff separately.

75. A year before he won the election which first made him Prime Minister. According to the *Guardian's* obituary, the ideas for the speech came from several committees in which Richard Crossman and Professor P.M.S.

Blackett played a crucial role.

76. Later called 'Landscape' alone - under the leadership of Professor Anne Beer.

77. Author's recorded interview with Anne Minors, 17th January 2007.

78. See website www.pam.org.my/Library/Tribute_to_the_Late_Dato_Ikmal_Hisham_Albakri.pdf -

79. See Harman and Minnis 2004.

80. It is prominent in Peter Reyner Banham's eponymous book published by Architectural Press, London, in 1966, the defining text of what has since been accepted historically as a movement.

81. The phrase of J.K. Galbraith, economist and author of *The Affluent Society*, 1958.

82. *Architectural Design* no. 9, September 1961, pp. 380-415 (edited by Pat Crooke). Park Hill received a major publication in *RIBA Journal* December 1962, pp. 447-469.

83. Editor Chris Napper, publisher Design in Sheffield, printed by The Castle Press, first issue summer/autumn 1964, 4 issues published, to 1966.

84. Womersley was chairman of both the local steering committee and the RIBA conference committee, and the conference was planned from 1958 onward. See Harper 1987, pp. 39-42.

85. Quoted in *The Daily Telegraph*, 18th July 1963.

86. A photograph of it was published in *Architects' Journal* 10th July 1963.

87. Nikolaus Pevsner et al. *Buildings of England, Yorkshire: West Riding*, Penguin, Harmondsworth, 1967 p. 460.

88. Building Committee Minutes for 19th November 1951, 8th January 1952.

89. See Jeremy Melvin, *F.R.S. Yorke and the Evolution of English Modernism*, Wiley-Academy, London 2003.

90. The Smithsons wound a cranked slab block around the hill contrasting the sloping ground with internal horizontal 'streets' as later executed at Park Hill. Stirling produced a Corbusian slab block with articulated wedge-shaped forms for lecture theatres.

91. Building Committee Minutes for 17th November 1953: university records.

92. Ibid, 6th March 1956.

93. Ibid, 18th August 1959.

94. The Building Committee minutes reveal many changes of mind and a rather pragmatic attitude, which would have made close tailoring of the building to specific departments very difficult. University records.

95. *'Take Gollins, Melvin, Ward and Partners' new university buildings at Sheffield in comparison. They are in the style of the 1930s - for that style, as we shall see, is by no means dead - and they are so much more neutral in expression without thereby in my opinion losing anything in aesthetic value. Their calm outline, their beautiful grouping and their precise detail reveal the excellence of their designer just as unmistakably as Stirling and Gowan's violent self-expression - and university buildings should perhaps convey calm and precision rather than ferocity. One thing in any case is certain. University buildings should be designed with a view to the user rather than the architect.'* Pevsner *The anti-pioneers*, radio broadcast published in *Pevsner, Nikolaus Pevsner on Art and Architecture* ed. Stephen Games, Methuen, London, 2002, p 300. This was also the occasion when Pevsner made the Freudian slip of referring to the Leicester Engineering

building as clad in blue bricks when in fact they are red. Arguably, the Leicester Building was in fact much more directly inspired by its functions: see Peter Blundell Jones and Eamonn Canniffe, *Modern Architecture Through Case Studies 1950-1990*, Architectural Press 2007, Chapter 6.

96. Geoffrey Broadbent, ed. *Signs symbols and architecture*, Wiley 1980, p. 121.

97. Author's recorded interview with John Allan, London, 31st October 2006.

98. Mentioned in a general article about the school unsigned but reportedly written by Architecture lecturers Alec Daykin and J. Marshall Jenkins: see *The Builder* October 11, 1963, pp. 789-793. In the *University of Sheffield Gazette* no. 545, November 1965, p. 58, John Needham reported that space in the Shearwood Road premises had restricted numbers to 150.

99. Obituary in the *Transactions of the Institute of Geographers* 1982, N.S.7 pp. 126-7.

100. *Turf Management*, January 1987.

101. Obituaries in *The Scotsman* 10th July 1977 and *Landscape Design,* September 1997.

102. Peter Reyner Banham, *The New Brutalism,* Architectural Press 1966.

103. Author's recorded interview with Andrew Beard, Sheffield, 10th November 2006.

104. Published by RIBA Press in 1992

105. Author's recorded interview with John Allan, 7th November 2006.

106. Note on undated first year drawing of four objects, the others being a screwdriver, curtain rail and lampshade, signed J.S. Allan, from Allan's original portfolio digitised by Peter Lathey and filed under 'Object drawing'.

107. Author's recorded interview with John Allan, London, 7th November 2006, and subsequent email.

108. Main course as counted from examination records.

109. Obituary typescript supplied by Kenneth Murta.

110. Gropius visited BDP in 1974, and wrote a letter of thanks that is in the Grenfell-Baines archive.

111. Rory Coonan in *The Independent*, 19th May 2003.

112. Author's recorded interview with Anne Minors, London, 17th January 2007.

113. Barry Maitland adds: *'During my time with the teaching practice we carried out some 50 or so architectural projects and competitions, including health projects (e.g. the Children's and Preventive Dentistry unit at Charles Clifford Dental Hospital), housing projects for Northern Counties Housing Association and other clients, pubs (e.g. Cow and Calf at Grenoside), industrial jobs, etc.. The projects ranged in size from small conversions to the largest, probably the Waterthorpe District Centre (now Crystal Peaks Centre) at Mosborough, which was won in a limited competition in 1981 and subsequently carried out by BDP.'* Email to the author July 2007.

114. They spent not only the usual fourth year of their training in this practice but also the fifth year, moving back into the school for a final sixth year; email from Barry Maitland July 2007.

115. Broadbent left in 1968, Tarn in 1969 and Jenkins in 1970, becoming the heads of schools of architecture in Portsmouth, Nottingham and Leeds respectively.

116. Author's recorded interview with David Cash at BDP Manchester 30th October 2006.

117. *RIBA Journal* February 1986, pp 41-43.

118. Author's recorded interview with John Allan who was active in the society.
119. From an obituary typescript supplied by Proctor.
120. Author's recorded interview with Anne Minors, 17th January 2007.
121. The debt was repaid in David Gosling, *Gordon Cullen: Visions of Urban Design* Wiley-Academy, 1996.
122. The key theoretical text is Aldo Rossi, *The Architecture of the City*, MIT Press 1982, which stressed the persistent forms of the city over their functions. The Kriers were best known for their drawings, published world wide, and Rob Krier's book *Urban Space*, Academy, 1979, was an architectural bestseller.
123. Stephen Proctor of Proctor and Matthews, one of the school's most distinguished alumni, produced a thesis project which swung between a fail and a distinction for lack of demonstrated architectural detail.
124. But Stephen Proctor and Andrew Matthews remember being taught by visiting Professor Michael Wilford in 1980-91 in their second and third years.
125. Listed in the University Calendar at one time or another as visiting critics over the years 1975 to 1989.
126. Verbal information from Peter Aldington, one of the longest serving critics.
127. Author's recorded interview with Greg Penoyre, 30th November 2006.
128. Aldington recalled a time when Peter Cook had to leave a day early and gave his on tape: *'a wonderful summing up, like a Radio Three broadcast'*, telephone conversation with the author, September 2006.
129. Author's recorded interview with David Cash, 30th October 2006.
130. Author's recorded interview with Simon Allford, 6th August 2007.
131. Conversation between Affleck and the author, 19th April 2007.
132 . Author's recorded interview with Bill Taylor, 24th November 2006.
133. Ibid.
134. Ibid.
135. Penn was the author of a series of distinguished private houses that have recently been rediscovered and exhibited, the drawings being in possession of the RIBA. Green worked for him from 1963-67.
136. Email from Cedric Green to the author, July 2007.
137. He went to Cincinnati as 'Eminent Scholar of Urban Design for the State of Ohio', but he was plagued by ill-health and died aged 67 in 2002. A further book *The Evolution of American Urban Design* was published posthumously in 2003.
138. Preface to the catalogue of the school's summer exhibition 1992, published by the school.
139. B. R. Lawson, and M. Phiri, *The Architectural Healthcare Environment and its Effects on Patient Health Outcomes*, London, The Stationery Office, 2003. ISBN 0-11-322480-X.
140. P.R. Tregenza and D. Loe, *The design of lighting,* E & FN Spon 1998 ISBN 0 419 20440 7; P.R. Tregenza *The design of interior circulation,* Crosby Lockwood Staples 1976, ISBN 0 258 96998 9.
141. See Alan Williams, *Architectural modelling as a form of research*, Architectural Research Quarterly, vol 6, no. 4, 2003, pp. 337-347.
142. Ph.Ds. were completed in the school on Sheffield's buildings for the steel industry by Alan Williams, on its markets and shopping by Jo Lintonbon, and on mid 20th century Sheffield planning by Alan Lewis.
143. See Peter Blundell Jones, Doina Petrescu, & Jeremy Till, eds. *Architecture and Participation*, Spon Press, London & New York, 2005.
144. All these figures come from the School's published Report to the RIBA visiting Board 1990.
145. Counting dual students and part-time staff as 0.5, omitting secretaries, technicians, computer programmer, and visiting professors: figures from exam records and staff handbook.
146. Undergraduate main course 249, Diploma course 94 = 343.
147. He claimed that the construction industry produces about 50% of all waste in the UK as against only 18% from domestic waste: all this from Till's inaugural lecture: see *Architects Journal* 17th February 2000, p. 54.
148. Author's recorded interview with Tom Vigar and others, May 2007.
149. Jamie Wakeford by email to the author, 24 th May 2007.
150. Author's recorded interview with Anne Minors, 17th January 2007.
151. Christine Hawley at the Bartlett was the first.
152. The Bureau of Design Research (BDR) was established in 2002 to make the School's extensive experience in research by design available to the wider community, giving independent advice, and offering a range of design-based services; from community-led regeneration and design projects to strategic projects for local and national government. After four years the BDR has established itself as a design-led research consultancy with over thirty funded nationwide projects in its portfolio.
153. Ruth Morrow, *Building clouds, drifting walls,* publication of the University of Sheffield School of Architecture 2003, pp. 10-12.
154. Rosie Parnell & Rachel Sara with Charles Doidge & Mark Parsons *The Crit, An Architecture Student's Handbook*, Architectural Press, Oxford 2000.
155. Ibid p. 5.
156. Written statement from Roger Plank, January 2007.
157. Ibid.
158. Ibid
159. Ibid.
160. Shankari Raj in an interview with the author May 2007.
161. Cover title of a special edition of *RIBA Journal*, April 1974, written by Malcolm MacEwen and based on his concurrent book. He reports that *'disenchantment set in'* in the mid 1960s and sees the failure of Ronan Point in 1968 as a turning point in the public mood. In a similar vein, though with a more environmental emphasis, Rolf Keller's powerful polemic *Bauen als Umweltzerstörung* (Building as pollution) was published in Zurich in 1973.

FACTORS IN THE EDUCATION AND DEVELOPMENT OF AN ARCHITECT:

INTRODUCTION:

These personal notes have been written with the object of conveying ideas on
the career of an architect which have occurred to me as I have practiced
architecture as an individual to begin with and as a member of many multi -
disciplinary design teams.

As points I have noticed along the way, they may strike you as having relevance
to your developing career and personality.   Even where they don't, it is
possible the contrast will serve to illuminate your thinking about your own
situation and philosophy.   I hope so.

1.   ON BEING AN ARCHITECT:

Contributing to the creative work of interpreting Society's building needs and
designing the buildings required is one of the most rewarding careers one
could choose.   However, contemporary developments in knowledge of building -
through from the understanding of social activities and objectives to
technologies of human and material resources - have widened the field of
available knowledge well beyond normal individual capacity.   To achieve truly
comprehensive building design, teams of specialists are needed today.

This development of separate specialist inputs can only be fully effective,
particularly in the wider meaning of architecture, if the inputs themselves
are truly integrated to realise their inter-active potential.   "The whole
greater than the sum of the parts".

How, or by whom, the integratory process is brought about is far less important
than the need for it to be achieved and particularly the realisation and
understanding in all members of the design team that successful integration
will inevitably require changes, even mutations of original individual design
contributions.   Just as this is a developing process for the design, it is
also a developing process for members of the design team.   Seeking for the
whole greater than the sum of the parts is itself a developing process from
which participants emerge matured - educated - by their experience.

Successful integration demands of each specialist a degree of awareness of his
fellow specialists' contributions, an awareness of the nature and content
embracing the essential principles and to some extent the philosophy of the
skill.   At present this is an area of education urgently requiring development,
a fact of which staff members of the Faculty of Architectural Studies at
Sheffield are well aware.

Considerable experience of building design has confirmed for me that while
specialist knowledge also requires supporting awareness in each individual,
it is necessary for each design team to contain at least one member with the
flair and knowledge to activate and inspire the integrating process.

-8-

Documents found in the school's archives.

219. (above) Part of a general policy statement issued to staff and students by George Grenfell-Baines at the start of
his headship in 1973.
220. (opposite) Third Year student design programme issued by Stephen Welsh, 1950.

THE UNIVERSITY OF SHEFFIELD.

DEPARTMENT OF ARCHITECTURE.

Easter Term.   THIRD YEAR.   Session 1950 -51.

Sketch Design.   A DOOR TO A GARDEN.

Your client asks you to design a door in the side of his
Renaissance palace near Florence.

The door will be used by your client and his friends as a
means of access to the formal garden.   The doorway, which should be
of stone, need not be highly elaborate; it should incorporate a
landing and stair or stairs which may, if you think fit, rise on
each side of a small fountain feature.

Drawings required:-

(1) A large perspective (or elevational drawing) in full colour
on an Imperial sheet.

(2) Plan, elevation and section to ⅛th inch scale.

Date of Issue. Tuesday, 24th. April, 1951. 9.30 a.m.

Date of Return. Wednesday, 25th. April, 9.30 a.m.

Site plan.   NOT TO SCALE

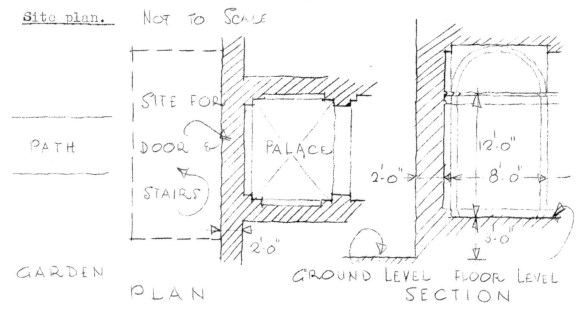

207

Sources of illustrations and photographs

Sheffield University Archives: Frontispiece, 1, 3, 5, 6, 19-26, 42, 43, 60-64, 55, 56, 69-72, 76, 77, 107, 114, 121, 148.

Sheffield City Archive/ Hadfield Cawkwell and Davidson: 2.

Peter Blundell Jones: 4, 7, 15, 17, 36, 73, 74, 81, 116, 151, 152, 176, 177, 184.

Sheffield University Library, Special Collections, Devey Collection: 8-11.

C.J. Innocent/ Cambridge University Press: 12-14.

Tim Wenham/ Robert Evans: 16.

Welsh family: 18

Alec Daykin: 27-35, 37-41.

Simon Allford: 44-47, 130-132.

Philip Toft: 48-52, 53-59.

Architectural Design/Academy: 67-68, 122, 123.

School of Architecture Archives, Photographer Peter Lathey: 75, 111-113, 115, 124-129, 133-147, 149, 150, 157-162, 168-175, 178-183, 185-190, 194-197, 204, 206, 207, 209, 212-220.

Faculty of Architectural Studies Prospectus 1965 (photocopy, no original found): 78-80.

John Allan: 82-106.

BDP Manchester: 108-110.

Anne Minors: 117-120.

Bryan Lawson: 153-155, 163.

Russell Light: 156.

Peter Tregenza: 164.

Olga Popovic: 165.

Jian Kang: 166.

Peter Szalapaj: 167.

Doina Petrescu: 205.

Jeremy Till: 191-193, 210-211.

Ruth Morrow: 198-201.

Mark Parsons: 202-203.

While every attempt has been made to trace the source and copyright of images used, the circumstances surrounding some of the older images are obscure. The author and publishers apologise for any copyright unknowingly infringed, and invite owners to identify themselves so that appropriate acknowledgement can be made in subsequent editions.